12 ETUDE-CAPRICES IN THE
Great Composers

AMY BARLOWE

Alfred Music
P.O. Box 10003
Van Nuys, CA 91410-0003
alfred.com

ISBN-10: 0-7390-6259-X
ISBN-13: 978-0-7390-6259-3

Painting by German genre painter, Otto Erdmann whose paintings show his fondness for the rococo period.

Dedication

With special thanks to my mother, whose meticulous and beautiful artwork has always inspired the best in me.

ACKNOWLEDGEMENTS

With fond remembrance and heartfelt thanks to my teachers, Ivan Galamian, Margaret Pardee, Louise Behrend, and Vincent Persichetti for sharing not only their technical and musical wisdom, but their great commitment to inspiring a lifelong passion for teaching and learning.

With much gratitude to my editor, Judi Bagnato, whose patience, kindness, and shared vision has made this book a reality.

With many thanks to my graphic designer, Elaine Padilla, my colleagues at the Meadowmount School of Music, "Historical Saranac Lake", Jessica Rauch, The Aaron Copland Fund, The University of Pennsylvania Library, The Library of Congress, Joseph Gold, Walter Watson, and the numerous individuals who so generously contributed their time and talents to the making of this book.

And, with love and great appreciation for the encouragement and help given to me by my husband, Alan Bodman, particularly in the final phase of editing each etude-caprice.

CONTENTS

PREFACE

The value of etudes (study pieces that serve to build and expand technique) is indisputable. A veritable staircase provided by the regimen of progressive etudes, from those of Wohlfahrt through the caprices of Paganini, has been climbed by the greatest violinists of our day and will undoubtedly continue to be ascended by generations of violinists to come. These primarily 19th century works have distinguished themselves through the centuries by establishing solid foundations for the technical demands encountered in the violin repertoire.

This being said, there are as many approaches to teaching technique as there are teachers, some more imaginative than others, some adhering rigidly to tradition, some creating their own blend. The best teaching, however, takes into account the individual needs of each student. Clues to these needs lie in an evaluation of learning styles. Often simply categorized as 1) visual, 2) aural, and 3) tactile, I have found, however, that the lines of demarcation between these learning types can frequently be somewhat indistinct. Factor in shorter attention spans, often the result of exhaustion from innumerable after school activities and electronically dominated life styles, and it can become an immense challenge to select technical material that will be of the greatest benefit to some of our students without boring them to tears.

The purposes and possibilities for uses of this collection of "etude-caprices" (study pieces which address not only technical, but also *musical* challenges) are many. In its most obvious role, it can serve as preparation for music by the composers on whose distinctive styles each "etude-caprice" is based. Believing that music from various periods is most effectively interpreted when articulations, bowings, fingerings, sonorities, phrasings and character reflect the socio-cultural environment of its origin, I have tried to capture the essence of each composer's life and times in *12 Etude-Caprices in the Styles of the Great Composers*. Before writing each etude-caprice, I would spend several days to a week immersing myself in the works of each composer and researching events and circumstances surrounding the creation of his music. As each etude-caprice emerged, I envisioned the technical means by which its interpretation could effectively depict its appropriate style. If a sense of elegance and decorum had defined the attitude of society, as it did in the classical period, it follows that the interpretation of music from this period, such as that of Joseph Haydn, would be one of refinement and simplicity. If, on the other hand, popular values of late 19th century France had been influenced by the philosopher, Henri Bergson, who stated that experience is "a series of qualitative changes which melt into and permeate one another, without outlines," one would be inclined to interpret the Etude-Caprice in the Style of Ravel in a manner that would convey the impression of flow in a kind of timeless haze. In so doing, I feel that the technique is fully integrated into the music, and as in any concert piece, one could not exist without the other.

In its conception, this book was never intended to replace the time-tested etudes that have transported so many of us from one level of ability to the next. In point of fact, for those students whose imaginations are primed, I enjoy encouraging the challenge of making something musical out of something which inherently is not. However, for some students, being the varied individuals that they are, this is not enough. *12 Etude-Caprices in the Styles of the Great Composers* will appeal to those who are not satisfied with exercises and study pieces for which they see no immediate relevance. Not only will they serve, in a sense, as prequels to the standard literature that students look forward to, but they should also help to build the technique necessary to eventually approach these future works, as well as those encountered in youth orchestras, in a much more rewarding manner.

The renowned violin pedagogue, Carl Flesch (1873–1944) believed that if students were compelled to spend too long on the technical apparatus of a piece, they would lose the essential means by which to express the music. "The technical level necessary for the rendition of the piece should have been reached before, by way of general technical studies." *12 Etude-Caprices in the Styles of the Great Composers* is yet another way in which to achieve readiness for the great works of the violin literature. By extracting technical and musical problems from these etude-caprices, no harm will come to the masterworks that we violinists cherish as our heritage. To help with this endeavor, I have included detailed practice guides following each etude-caprice. It is my hope that these will reinforce practice tools and foster new discoveries. Additionally, I would highly encourage students to explore the workings of the great composers' minds by researching elements from their environments and personalities that can be incorporated into their respective styles. The more knowledge accrued in this regard, the more interesting and enjoyable will be the study and performances of these works. *12 Etude-Caprices in the Styles of the Great Composers* can most definitely be used as a supplement, but with the development of the essential technique and musicianship for rendering each etude-caprice playable, the student, if so inclined, can also seek to transform these etude-caprices or "concert studies" into "concert pieces," as they can easily find a place on recital programs.

1. In the Style of Vivaldi

Amy Barlowe

IN THE STYLE OF
Vivaldi

 TECHNICAL ELEMENTS

Detaché
Martelé
Rapid string crossings
Wrist flexibility
Intonation

 MUSICAL ELEMENTS

Phrase direction
Dynamics
Vibrato
Baroque style

PRACTICE GUIDE

Section 1

Ⓐ **mm. 1, 2, 3, 4** – This etude-caprice can be used as a resource for establishing the frame for a relaxed left hand posture. Extract the four octaves from the first four measures. Practice them individually. The elbow should be pulled slightly to the right, allowing the wrist to remain straight and encouraging the arch of the 4th finger. There should be no reach upwards to find the top note of the octave. Then open the hand, slightly pulling back the first finger before placing it an octave below. The perfect octave should sound like one note. (See Appendix II for techniques to improve intonation.) When the intonation is secure, play the C octave with one long, slow bow. Stop at the point. Lifting the fingers just slightly, but treating them as a unit, swing the elbow slightly to the left, and shift down to the E octave. Play this octave on a long, slow up bow and stop. Lighten the fingers, and once again treating them as a unit, come around the violin by pulling the arm slightly to the right, making the shift to the G octaves. When dependably in tune, pull a long, slow down bow, and stop. Finally, swing the elbow a tiny bit to the left, and shift down to the 2nd position C octave. Pull a long, slow up bow, and stop. A couple of things to remember: Never squeeze the neck of the violin. Maintain the left hand posture by shifting with the whole arm and treating the octaves as units rather than individual fingers.

Ⓑ **mm. 1, 2, 3, 4** – When the frame of the hand is set for this etude-caprice, break the octaves as written. Put a slight space between the notes of each octave to articulate them. Use more bow on the first note of each octave and less on the second to give more importance to the first. (The analogy of dropping a ball, where the second bounce does not reach the level of the first, helps to explain this concept.) Next, begin to add the scale passages one at a time within the context of each frame. The posture of the left hand should not be altered. Learn each pattern. (See Appendix IV.) If helpful, reverse the scales to secure the intervals.

Ⓒ This is primarily an upper half bow piece. Establish the vital, energetic character right away, and keep it throughout this etude-caprice!

D Dynamics were seldom written into baroque music. It was expected that the well trained musicians of this period would abide by the conventions of the day, so markings of this nature were not necessary. To assist those with less experience, however, dynamics are indicated in this etude-caprice. Keep in mind that markings of any kind are most useful when they ignite the imagination.

E Terrace the dynamics. Follow the line while terracing by the sequence. Crescendo by the measure, but allow the sixteenth note patterns to diminuendo slightly within this framework. (To diminuendo on the detaché, gradually reduce the bow towards the middle.)

F **mm. 5, 6** – Practice the string crossings on the open D and A strings in the middle of the bow first with little "stop bows." Exaggerating the motions, drop the wrist from the hand, making it "low" for the low string; then raise the wrist, making it "high" for the high string. (This can be practiced without a violin before starting.) When this is easy, try smooth small detaché strokes. Use only the amount of bow it takes to make the crossing. Next, practice the notes that comprise the string crossings in this etude-caprice as double stops in order to polish the intonation. (See Appendix V for tips on practicing double stops.) When the intonation is solid, apply the flexible wrist to the passage as written. Start very slowly. Be sure the flexibility remains as the tempo is built. As the speed increases and the exaggeration diminishes proportionally, a fluid flexibility will develop. Remember: smaller motions require smaller muscle groups. There is no need to use the whole arm to make a little string crossing. Always seek efficiency, ease and natural elegance.

G **m. 6** – For articulation appropriate to this style, slightly separate the eighth notes in beats 3 and 4. Keep the vibrato going in order to keep it from sounding dry.

Caricature of Vivaldi by P.L.Ghezzi, Rome (1723)

Section 2

A **m. 7, 8, 9** – Start with less bow in the middle. To crescendo, open up the bow, using more (in the upper half) for every sequence.

B **m. 7** – When crossing the string for only one note, be sure to use a flexible wrist (not the arm) for efficiency. *Reminder: small motions require smaller muscle groups to look and sound easy and natural.*

C **mm. 7 through 10** – Make ½ steps wide when using the same finger chromatically. Alter the positions of the fingers from squared to slightly extended on chromatic half steps (for example, when moving from the F-natural to the F-sharp and the G-natural to the G-sharp).

D Phrase by the sequence and with the shape of the line. Test phrasing by placing an enormous hole between phrases. If the phrases still make sense, they work. As an example, in m. 7, try phrasing after the C of the 2nd beat. Treating the E as a pick up to the next pattern, could give more interest to the phrase than starting each phrase predictably at the beginning of every measure. Build sextuplets using the aforementioned steps.

Modern day look at a canal in Venice, Italy, where Vivaldi was born.
(Photograph, Nino Barbieri)

Section 3

A **m. 10 through the first 2 beats of m. 11** – With each sequence, reduce the bow more and more to the middle. This will enable each descending pattern to diminuendo in accordance with the line.

B Phrase by the sequence and follow the shape of the line to define the pattern.

C **m. 11 (middle) through m. 13 (middle)** – Bring out the melody on top as though there were two voices. A touch of vibrato will help. Repeated notes are accompaniment, so play them with less bow and consequently, less sound.

Section 4

A m. 13 (middle) through m. 15 – For an easy, relaxed detaché stroke, open and close the inside elbow enough to stay on the sounding point. Keep the bow fingers quiet and bend the wrist towards the nose. Always practice on open string equivalents to improve the sound quality.

B mm. 14, 15 – Show dynamics by very subtly reducing and increasing the amounts of bow in the upper half according to the shape of the line. Shaping with dynamics encourages the development of relationships between notes. It also fosters an awareness of phrase direction.

NOTE: When the intonation is accurate and secure, the entire etude-caprice can be made more vibrant by keeping the left hand slightly active and adding a touch of vibrato throughout. Place the fingers closer to the nail, rather than their pads, to create a vibrato appropriate to this style of music. Add a little stronger vibrato to enhance important notes.

The Ospedale della Pieta, a renowned orphanage and music school for girls, where Vivaldi did much of his composing and served as master violin teacher from 1704 to 1740.

Section 5

A mm. 16, 17 – Practice in double stops first. (See Appendix V.)

B mm. 16, 17 – Keep the wrist flexible on string crossings. (See Section 1/F.) Crescendo by the sequence using more bow for each pattern. With a slight flick of the wrist and a touch of vibrato, pick out the melody line on the bottom.

Section 6

A mm. 18, 19 – Play the eighth notes like martelés but with less pinch at the beginning of each stroke. Make the string crossings clean. Practice crossing the strings silently by simply sitting the bow on the string and changing elbow levels. When adding the horizontal motion required by the stroke, be sure to prepare the elbow level. The elbow and stick levels should match. The easiest places to check levels are at the middle and the heel of the bow. Keep one elbow level per string.

B mm. 18, 19 – Keep vibrato going to eliminate dryness.

C mm. 18, 19 – Shape dynamically with the line.

Section 7

A mm. 20, 21, 22, 23 – Practice in double stops first.

B mm. 20, 21 – Play the slurs with stops between each note to feel the elbow levels. (See Appendix II for "Stop Bow Method".) Keep the triplets very even. Be careful that the middle notes of every triplet do not get lost by passing over them too quickly. (If this is a problem, see Appendix IV for rhythmic practice tools.)

C mm. 20, 21 – Swing arm like a pendulum to connect notes across the strings. Add vibrato.

D mm. 22, 23 – Build sextuplets using the aforementioned steps. Be sure that both of the repeated top notes sound evenly.

E mm. 20, 21, 22, 23 – Keep the bow moving. Add the long swells when the rhythm is accurate and the notes are even.

Section 8

A mm. 24, 25 (to middle) – Check the coordination of the detaché. (See Appendix IV.) The inside elbow should open and close almost mechanically. The fingers should come down just before the bow moves so that the detaché sounds clean.

B mm. 24, 25 (to middle) – When secure, vary the amount of detaché to help shape the phrase musically.

Section 9

A m. 25 (middle) through m. 28 – Start with little bows in the middle. Remember to pick out the melody line with a snap of the wrist and a touch of vibrato. Play less on the repeated notes, which are accompaniment.

B m. 25 (middle) through m. 28 – Open the bow from the inside elbow to make a dramatic crescendo as the line ascends to m. 29.

C m. 29 – Slightly separate the top A from the bottom A. As mentioned earlier, the first A will have more bow than the second to create the diminuendo.

D m. 29 – Begin the 3rd beat with little bow. Open it up, making a crescendo to the end of the measure, and breathe to set up the restatement of the first theme, this time in piano.

JUDITHA TRIUMPHANS
DEVICTA HOLOFERNIS BARBARIE
Sacrum Militare Oratorium
HISCE BELLI TEMPORIBUS
A Psalentium Virginum Choro
IN TEMPLO PIETATIS CANENDUM
JACOBI CASSETTI EQ.
METRICE' VOTIS EXPRESSVM.
Piissimis ipsius Orphanodochii PRÆSI-
DENTIBVS ac GUBERNATORIBUS
submisse Dicatum .
MUSICE' EXPRESSUM
Ab Admod. Rev. D.
ANTONIO VIVALDI

VENETIIS , MDCCXVI.
Apud Bartholomæum Occhium, sub signo S. Dominici.
SUPERIORUM PERMISSU.

Frontispiece for first edition of Vivaldi's first great oratorio, Juditha Triumphans.

Most likely due to either ill health or an earthquake that occurred on the day of his birth, the infant Vivaldi was immediately baptized in the Church of San Giovanni Battista in Bragora, Venice, Italy.

Section 10

A mm. 32, 33, 34, 35 – Use the same articulations as those used in the opening of the etude-caprice.

B mm. 32, 33, 34, 35 – Make the dynamics even more dramatic than those used at the beginning.

C mm. 34, 35 – Separate and vibrate the eighth notes as well as the quarters.

D mm. 32, 33, 34, 35 – Keep the energy all the way to the end!

Detail from *APOTHEOSE DER SPANISCHEN KÖNIGSFAMILIE*
G.B. Tiepolo (1762–1766)

2. In the Style of Bach

Amy Barlowe

Allegro ma non troppo

12

IN THE STYLE OF
Bach

TECHNICAL ELEMENTS

Variable Detaché
Double stops
Wrist flexibility
Turned chords

MUSICAL FEATURES

Polyphony
Dynamics
Phrase direction
Rhythmic vitality

PRACTICE GUIDE

Section 1

A   m. 1, 2 – Using detaché bow strokes not too close to the bridge, start the first three-note gesture with more bow in the upper half and reduce towards the middle of the bow to diminuendo slightly. This will give more importance to the downbeat. *In order to keep the steady rhythmic pulse inherent in the style of this etude-caprice, always hear sixteenth notes wherever there are rests.* Shape the melody by bringing out the lower voice and subordinating the open A's. A flexible wrist (lower for the low string and higher for the high string) will help pick out the melodic notes. Practice the string crossings in an exaggerated manner first. (See Vivaldi etude-caprice 1/F.) Adding a touch of vibrato and some subtle dynamic shaping on the melodic notes in the 3rd and 4th beats will help point the way to the C-sharp downbeat of m. 2. Vibrate the 4th finger A at the beginning of the 3rd beat of m. 2 to show its importance.

B   Give the sixteenth notes vibrancy in this etude-caprice by keeping the left hand active with just a touch of vibrato.

C   When the detaché stroke is reliable, try varying the amount of bow on these strokes to help shape the lines. Baroque music rarely had dynamics written into parts because composers expected their well trained musicians to employ the conventions of the time. The dynamics appearing in the music are only guidelines and suggestions. The louder dynamics will require more bow than the softer ones. But "reading between the lines" is a valuable endeavor. The more interesting the shapes are, the better. For example, when a line ascends, try using more bow from the middle towards the point to crescendo. When the line descends, reduce the bow back to the middle to diminuendo. Use imagination to create compelling dynamic ideas.

D   m. 3 – This measure is a diminutive version of the first measure. Play it with the same shapes but softly, using less bow in the middle.

Section 2

A **m. 5, 6** – Polyphonic music is that which has multiple voices. Look for two voices hidden in these measures. With subtlety, differentiate between them. The double stop D-F on the first beat of m. 5, and the C-sharp and D at the beginnings of the 3rd and 4th beats respectively, could be leading towards the double stop E-G on the down beat of m. 6 constituting one of those two voices. The remaining notes might be thought of as being more accompanimental and can be treated as such. Practice the two voices individually, at first, to understand their shapes. When they make sense, combine them. Detecting and revealing melodic skeletons in music of this nature gives much more interest to its performance.

B **m. 7, 8** – Notice how the two voices have traded places. In mm. 5 and 6, the melody seemed to be in the top voice. In mm. 7 and 8, the melody resides in the bass. Give the low strings at the beginnings of the 1st and 3rd beats more resonance, much like the pedals of an organ.

C Crescendo to the súbito piano at the beginning of m. 9.

Bach was organist at St. Thomas Church in Leipzig.

Section 3

A Notice how the two voices interact within this section. Work very carefully on the intonation of the double stops to help bring out the melodic voice convincingly. (See Appendix V for hints on improving the intonation and a general approach to double stops.) Vibrate the double stops and show their direction. Subordinate the less important voice, but always shape imaginatively. Use sounding point and bow speed changes to help distinguish between the two voices. For example, the voice with double stops could be played with a little more bow, slightly faster, lighter and farther from the bridge. For contrast, the other voice could use a little less bow and bow speed and be played slightly closer to the bridge.

B Be sure to balance on both strings equally when playing double stops.

C Separate the eighth notes stylistically, but give them a little vibrato to keep them from sounding too dry.

D Terrace the dynamics in this section, but also be sure to shape within the context of each dynamic level. Vary the lengths of detaché strokes for this purpose.

Original manuscript for Bach's Adagio from his solo violin sonata in G minor.

Section 4

A Since the melody is in the bottom voice throughout this section, it will be necessary to turn the chords downwards in order to end on the melodic note. Anticipate the downbeat of measure 13 with the top two notes (D and F) of the chord. With relaxed fingers and a continuous half moon motion, roll from those top two notes down to the D, arriving in time for the downbeat. Be sure not to play too heavily on the D and F as they are part of the top voice which will require slightly faster, lighter bow strokes.

B Reminder: Differentiate between voices and use a flexible wrist for string crossings throughout this section.

C **m. 15** – Use less bow towards the middle for an effective echo.

D **m. 16** – Work towards a lower portion of the bow during the last four sixteenths of this measure. After the last sixteenth note (open A) and at approximately the lowest quarter of the bow, with curved fingers, lift slightly in preparation for the chord that begins Section 5.

Section 5

A Because this section starts forte with a sense of nobility, give more equal importance to both voices. Approaching horizontally from slightly above the strings, try playing all three notes of the chords at once with a warm resonant sound. Never be heavy or harsh with your chords. (Practice on open string equivalents first. See Appendix VI.) Remember to start chords by pulling slightly "in", and *do not* play too close to the bridge. Keep the fingers flexible while pulling with the arm. Start the stroke with the upper arm. It is extremely important to resist the temptation to press in order to get all three notes of the chords to speak. Instead, pull the sound so all three strings vibrate as long as they can. (The amount of bow used will be determined, in part, by the tempo. As always, use the ear to decide if the sound quality is compromised by too little or too much bow speed.) If a little roll from lower to upper strings works best, this may require the slightest anticipation of the lower note to keep rhythmically secure. Be sure to keep the bow moving.

B Warning: Do not let chords distort the rhythmic accuracy of the sixteenth note voice.

C Add vibrato to chords when the intonation is secure and they sound easy and open.

D Vary the amount of detaché used for the moving voice (sixteenth notes) in relation to the dynamic level and shape of the line.

E Make a dramatic crescendo from the last beat of m. 19 through the forte in the 3rd beat of m. 20.

Section 6

A mm. 21, 22 – Contrast the two voices through the use of dynamics, sounding point changes, shaping and articulation. Work on one voice at a time until goals are met. The more prominent voice requires warm, resonant chords. Understand the horizontal intervallic finger relationships from one string to the next when a chord is preceded by a double stop. (See Appendix V.)

B mm. 21, 22 – Notice that the secondary voice is distinguished by the dots that are placed above its eighth notes as well as the softer dynamic. Try playing these short and light, with a slightly faster bow speed farther from the bridge, to differentiate this voice even more. Warning: Do not slow down!

C mm. 23, 24 – Balance the voices more in these two measures, and with a rich, vibrated sound on the G string, emphasize and give direction to the last three eighth notes in the crescendo at the end of m. 24 in order to set up a dramatic return to the restatement.

Section 7

A Like the beginning, be sure to keep sixteenth notes in mind during the rests. Make the dynamics and shaping even more dramatic than they were to start the piece. As with life's experiences, everything is richer and more meaningful the second time around. Remember to keep the sixteenth notes vibrant with lots of shape, energy and a touch of vibrato.

Section 8

A Play this section as a bold and decisive affirmation of all that has come before. Keep the energy through the end!

B m. 31 – The drama of the four note chord on the 2nd beat of this measure can be enhanced with a sense of timing. Borrow just enough time from the open A before it, anticipate and break that chord just enough to arrive dramatically on the 2nd beat of the measure without distorting any of the following sixteenth notes.

C m. 32 – Gradually broaden this last measure, ending on rich and vibrant unison D's. (Do not over vibrate the unison, for the sake of good intonation.) After taking the bow off the string, keep the vibrato going for as long as the sound remains spinning in the air.

3. In the Style of Handel

Amy Barlowe

IN THE STYLE OF
Handel

TECHNICAL ELEMENTS

Legato bow changes
Articulations
Intonation
Sounding point changes
Trills

MUSICAL ELEMENTS

Vibrato
Phrasing
Dynamics
Direction
Baroque style

PRACTICE GUIDE

Section 1

A This etude-caprice can suggest a stylized sarabande, a baroque dance in which the second beat is characteristically slightly heavier than the first. Vary the bow speeds and sounding points. For example, in the case of the dotted quarter note on the second beat of m. 1, use a little slower bow, closer to the bridge, with slightly more weight. (See Appendix III for information about sounding points.)

B **mm. 3, 4** – The slur with dashes over the quarter notes, C and B, indicates an editorial marking for slight separation, or portato. A touch of vibrato will carry the sound through the separation, avoiding dryness. (If there were an urtext [original] edition of this etude-caprice and it had actually been written in the Baroque period, the bowing for this figure would most likely have been separate.) The two successive up bows allow the first four-bar phrase to end with elegance, especially when the last down bow (in m. 4) is followed by a lighter up bow. With this in mind, match the written articulation with the sound of two separate bows.

C **m. 4** – Start the trill from above, taking care to trill to a C natural. Be sure the trill is even and not too fast.

D Keep the vibrato going throughout the etude-caprice. Vary its widths so that even the sixteenth notes stay enlivened by a touch of vibrato.

E Many Baroque composers were quite religious. Often, composers of this period would use their writing to express their beliefs by encouraging the use of dynamics that followed their musical lines. For example, rising lines represented an ascent to heaven, while descending lines would depict the reverse. Although dynamics reflected the conventions of the day and were usually left to the taste and expertise of the performer, suggestions are provided in this etude-caprice. Always use plenty of dynamic contrast to give the most interest to performances.

ℱ m. 9 – Be careful to avoid the temptation to over-hold the dotted eighth note in the last beat of this measure.

Section 2

A m. 10, 11 – Shift the half step up to second position and back down to first by lightening the finger before the shift, coming around with the arm, and shifting with the thumb and whole arm. Check the intonation with as many open strings as possible.

B Crescendo and diminuendo by sequences.

C m. 14 – The swell on the dotted quarter A is reminiscent of the baroque messa di voce. Deriving from vocal music, this tool gave motion to longer notes.

D m. 15 – Keep a loose elbow on the two detaché sixteenth notes that appear between slurs. Once again, trill evenly and not too quickly.

Engraving: Houses of Parliament from the River, in the time of Charles II (during Handel's lifetime)

Section 3

A mm. 18, 19 – Separate the eighth notes slightly, imitating the natural tendency of the baroque bow to lighten slightly at the end of a stroke.

B m. 20 – Phrase off a bit on the A at the end of the four-bar phrase by slowing and lightening the bow slightly.

C mm. 21, 24 – Because of the differences in bow speed between the dotted notes and the quicker notes that follow, be very careful not to accent the open E's after the dotted notes. To compensate for the natural brightness of the open E's as well as their shorter note values, play them with lighter and somewhat faster bows farther away from the bridge. Listen to the quality of the sound to determine the speed and sounding point that work best.

D mm. 22, 23, 24 – For the mixed bowings (detaché and legato combinations), use appropriate sounding points to maintain the quality of sound. (See Appendix III.) Be sure to bring out the melody in the bass quite elegantly. A touch of vibrato will help.

Handel in his youth

Section 4

A mm. 26 through 30 – Play the eighth notes slightly separated from each other. Vibrate, though, in order to keep the sound spinning.

B m. 29 – Watch the intonation on 2nd fingers since they move from low to high (G to C-sharp). If there is a problem, practice the same wide half step with the 2nd finger on one string (e.g. G to G-sharp) keeping the finger square for G and extending it for the G-sharp. (The shape of the finger will be slightly extended for the chromatically altered note.) Then apply this to the original notes on both strings.

C mm. 31, 32, 33 – Be careful to count the ties accurately. Try to make these measures a little darker and more passionate with dynamics, bow speeds, sounding points, vibrato and soul.

mm. 34, 35 – Use changes of sounding points to help build the crescendo and brighten the return to the first theme. In this case, hold the bow hand slightly in, allowing the contact point for the down bow slurs to remain closer to the bridge. This, in turn, enables the up bow detachés to start on their sounding point, which would be slightly farther away from the bridge.

Section 5

Treat this section as an ornamental version of the opening six measures. The sixteenths are somewhat decorative. Make them beautiful but not too important, with a touch of vibrato, dynamic shape and direction. Once again, keep the sarabande in mind.

Handel's house in Halle, the city where he was born.
(Photograph, Tamas Szalai)

Section 6

Increase the amount of bow mainly in the upper half to crescendo for a dramatic ending.

Sounding point changes will help balance the sound to compensate for differences in bow speed. Use vibrato to outline the melody.

Always check bow speeds and sounding points for a good core to the sound.

mm. 46, 47 – Placing the appoggiatura on the beat will help give the characteristic added weight to the second beat of m. 46. Remember to trill evenly and not too fast. The trill can be stopped on the 3rd beat to give the ending more solidity. Broaden the last two beats leading to the final downbeat. While keeping the vibrato going, lift the slightest bit between mm. 46 and 47 in order to drop and pull the last note with finality. To keep the sound spinning, vibrate even after the bow comes off the string at the close of this etude-caprice.

Detail from *THE SWING*
Jean-Honoré Fragonard (1767–1768)

4. In the Style of Haydn

Amy Barlowe

In the Style of
Haydn

Technical Elements

Off string bowings
Sounding points
Rhythmic accuracy
Syncopation

Musical Features

Vibrato
Phrasing
Dynamics
Direction
Classical style

Practice Guide

Section 1

A   **mm. 1, 2** – In general, at approximately the balance point of the stick and from not too great a height above the string, toss the bow on the strings for the spiccato notes. (Take the last eighth note of m. 1 off after starting from the string, as it is preceded by a detaché note.) Fingers should be flexible, curving slightly for each up bow spiccato. Let the resiliency of the stick do the work as the bow bounces on the string. Vibrate for resonance. Give the syncopated notes in these two measures slight accentuation to show the direction and set the tone for this highly spirited etude-caprice.

B   **m. 3** – The elegance and refinement of the classical style is often imparted through an almost imperceptible lightening of the bow particularly at the ends of two note slurs.

C   Use appropriate sounding points throughout this etude-caprice to give focus and balance to the sounds created by bow speeds that are derived from the wide variety of mixed bowings employed. (See Appendix III.)

D   **m. 6** – Separate slightly (on the string) the last two eighth notes in this measure. To keep them from sounding too dry, give them a little vibrato.

E   **m. 7** – Start the trill from above to impart grace.

F   **m. 8** – Phrase off the F-sharp without playing through the rest, but keep vibrating even when the bow comes off the string.

Section 2

A Be aware of sounding points for the mixed bowings that occur in this section. The slur and spiccato combinations should not use too much bow and will be most comfortable below the middle, close to the balance point. (See Appendix III.)

B m. 10 – Leave the fingers down as long as possible, and recognize intervals (5ths, in this case) across the fingerboard. Be aware that the 4th finger B's may want to pull up the 2nd fingers, if not treated with care. Come around, and shift from G to B with the whole arm. (See Appendix II regarding shifting.)

C m. 11 – Make spiccato D's ring with a round sound. Give them direction and a little vibrato for extra charm.

D mm. 12 and 15 – The detaché can be sprung slightly to accommodate the diminuendo and give more variety. In slow motion, the tiniest squeeze with the index finger will give the sensation of sinking just the slightest bit into and coming right out of the string in a dish-like manner. In this etude-caprice, this "sprung detaché" will be most effective in softer dynamics or to assist in diminuendos. It can also be used to blend gradually into spiccato for more variety and character, as in mm. 15 and 20. (Use open strings and the open string equivalents to practice blends from one bow stroke to another.)

Haydn was born in this home in Rohrau, Austria.

E Remember to follow the shape of the lines for dynamics, and keep vibrato going for a lively sound.

Section 3

A Play mm. 18 and 20 on the string in detaché, and contrast them with the use of spiccato for the eighth notes in the echo at m. 22. (Reminder: The end of m. 20 can blend to spiccato. Practice blends on open string equivalents.) When playing spiccato, remember that the fingers are the guides, and the forearm is the motion. Let the bow do the work. In this case do not start from too high above the string, and play slightly on the side of the bow hair, with the hair facing inward. Spiccatos of this nature work well just below the middle of the bow. (Note: The more direct the stick is above the hair, the crisper the sound will be. Imagine the sound you want for the spiccatos, and experiment with the amount of hair and location for dropping the bow.)

B mm. 21, 22, 23, 24 – Using a slur and spiccato combination, be sure to show the direction of this four-bar phrase. Crescendo to its top in order to contrast this section with the more lyrical material at Section 4

C m. 24 – Remember to vibrate the 4th finger D and let the vibrato keep going as long as the quarter note sounds. Use the rest at the end of the measure to get ready for the upcoming character change occurring at the bridge to the development section.

Section 4

A mm. 25, 27, 29, 31 – Give every octave leap more energy and direction. Vibrate well on 4th fingers. (If need be, practice 4th finger vibrato scales on every string as a strengthening exercise. If 4th fingers are particularly weak, do only a small amount of this kind of practice to start, building with rhythms every day. See Appendix IV.) Be careful not to over hold the ties.

B mm. 26, 28, 30 – In this case, trill from the note with precision. Very slightly whip or pinch the very beginning of each trill for clarity of articulation.

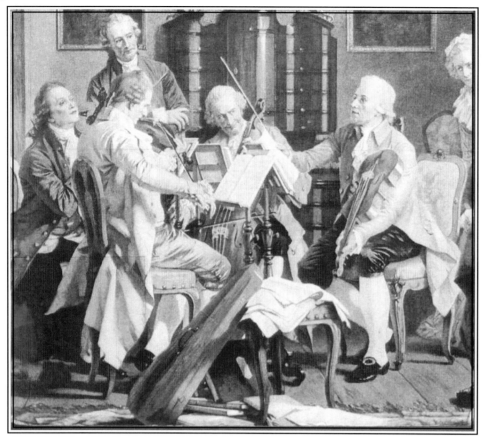

Haydn playing string quartets

ℭ mm. 33 (middle), 34, 35, 36 – Make dotted rhythms crisp. Practice in slow motion first. Count the four sixteenths in each figure in order to avoid playing triplets. Lighten the bow slightly at the end of the dotted eighth notes. Get back into the string again for the quick staccato sixteenth notes. Keep fingers on the bow flexible as they need to help with the short staccatos. Build the tempo, maintaining the precision. Add vibrato and dynamics.

𝕯 m. 38 – After arriving in third position, stay there. Keep 4th finger D planted until 1st finger is pulled back and ready to play the G#. Lift 1st finger only slightly to move it to the A at the beginning of m. 39.

ℰ m. 39 – A slight pairing of the two up bow slurs is stylistic. Lighten the ends of each. Encourage these pairs to keep the sense of direction headed towards the downbeat of m. 42.

ℱ m. 40 – Treat the grace note F-sharp, before the long trill, as an accented appoggiatura. Lean on it slightly as it borrows time from the note it precedes. Trill evenly and not too fast for the classical style. Change the bow imperceptibly before the nachschlag (end of the trill) which should point to the close of the phrase. Be sure to arrive on the downbeat of m. 41 exactly on time. When practicing a figure such as this one, use the following steps for accuracy, elegance and dependability:

1. Practice without any ornaments.

2. One at a time, take the first ornament you see. Play the note without ornamenting but hear inside where that particular ornament will be.

3. Play that ornament, the note that follows and its resolution. Be sure to count the main note accurately.

4. Repeat steps 1, 2 and 3 with all subsequent ornaments, adding one ornament at a time. It is especially important to have heard the ornament in the mind's ear before attempting to play it.

5. Play the whole figure in context.

Haydn spent his last years in this house in Vienna.

Section 5 & 6

A Refer to the opening of this etude-caprice for articulation suggestions. Section 5 begins a short development, the nature of which is somewhat more serious than the etude-caprice's outer sections, although the character of this work really reflects "Papa" Haydn's amiable personality.

B The sixteenth notes at Section 6 will benefit by being practiced in a variety of rhythms and bowings. (See Appendix IV.) In this way intonation, coordination and general technical ease can be secured.

C **mm. 58 through 64** – are comprised, once again, of bridge material. This time, however, the octaves are reversed, descending perhaps with a sense of pathos, be it short-lived. Also take note of the dashes (rather than dots) that appear just below the sixteenths of the hooked figures. Keep the rhythm accurate, but do not play the sixteenth notes quite as crisply as before. Held back only slightly with the poco ritard of m. 63, and having overcome the unrest of the previous section, these dotted rhythms should lead rather triumphantly back to the restatement.

View from the stage of Haydnsaal in Eisenstadt's Esterházy Palace where many of Haydn's works were premiered. One of the most acoustically perfect concert halls in the world.

Eszterháza Palace. As Kapellmeister to one of Austria's most prominent families, Haydn spent much time in this isolated setting while yearning for Vienna.

Section 7

A Play the return of the first theme with exuberance, making articulations and shapes tastefully more pronounced.

B **mm. 73 through 76** – Give the spiccato bowings more bounce, keeping these measures soft and alive.

C **mm. 77, 78** – Bring out the swell in these two measures in order to set up the last crescendo. Detach the last two eighth notes of m. 77, giving the B a little more bow than the G-sharp in accordance with the diminuendo.

D **mm. 79, 80** – Play these measures on the string, separating slightly to articulate the syncopation and give life to the eighth notes. Keep the bow moving and the vibrato going.

E **m. 82** – Accent the appoggiatura, and point the trill towards the downbeat of the penultimate measure.

F **m. 83, 84** – Try not to break the chords. Retake with a circular motion. (See Appendix VI.) In the final measure, take the bow off the strings with an elegant follow-through. Vibrate as long as the sound of the last chord remains spinning in the air!

5. In the Style of Mozart

Amy Barlowe

In the Style of

Mozart

 ### TECHNICAL ELEMENTS
Chords
Sounding point changes
Bow organization
Rhythm

 ### MUSICAL FEATURES
Characters
Phrasing
Dynamics
Vibrato
Classical style

PRACTICE GUIDE

Section 1

A When learning this etude-caprice, invent an operatic story complete with characters and scenery inspired by the musical ideas and gestures. The more imagination, the better!

B Immediately capture the drama of the first theme with the motion of the G minor chord and the direction of the first four-bar phrase. Spend plenty of time on this first chord, getting it to sound as warm and open as possible. Practice on open strings first. Approach the chord with flexible fingers from a counter-clockwise circle in the air and not too close to the bridge. (See Appendix VI for additional help.) Keep the shoulder down and the bow moving. Slightly anticipate the down beat of the first measure with the two lower notes. The top two notes should arrive exactly on the first beat of m. 1. Repeat with the actual notes of the chord, taking care to play them in tune with a resonant sound. When this is dependable, begin the etude-caprice.

C Add a vivacious classical vibrato to the chords (a little closer to the nail with a finger that is not too flat). Imagine a heartbeat to gauge the speed and width of vibrato. In this case, the opening phrase is asking for a stronger, faster vibrato. When taking the bow off the string for the rest at the end of m. 4, keep the vibrato going as long as the sound remains in the air.

An anonymous 19th century watercolorist painted this scene from Act I of Mozart's comic opera, The Marriage of Figaro.

m. 2 – Stylistically, lift slightly between the two D's. Keep the elbow loose for the two separate detaché notes between the slurs.

m. 5 – This measure would benefit from a more concentrated amount of bow and the understanding of sounding point changes. (See Appendix III.) Play the spiccato lower in the bow than where the down bow slurs finish. In order to do this, anticipate the up bow by catching it on the way back to the down bow. This graceful motion will prevent unwanted accents and stiffness.

m. 6 – Follow the line for dynamics.

m. 7,8 – Be careful not to accent the open A sixteenth note following the three-note slur at the end of the measure. Lighten it, but get back in the string for the beginning of m. 8. Count the 2nd and 4th beats of m. 8 in sixteenths in order to understand where the thirty-seconds fit.

m. 9 – Get a vibrant detaché (not too close to the bridge) for the forte sixteenth notes in the first two beats of this measure. Add a little extra weight on the slur that falls on the 3rd beat. (See Appendix III.) Vibrato will also give the passage much more life.

m. 11 – Remember to keep the vibrato going after taking the bow off of the string. Think ahead, imagining the upcoming character change.

The touring Mozart family, Leopold, Wolfgang, and Nannerl, in a watercolor painting from about 1763 by Carmontelle

Section 2

Without slowing, change the character. A slightly wider, slower but elegant vibrato and a slower bow that has moved a little closer to the bridge will create the warm, sweet sound that is desirable. Always imagine the sound first. (When the note values get smaller, causing the bow to move faster, the sounding point will once again move away from the bridge.)

m. 13 – Wide half steps between the C-sharp and C-natural will help the intonation.

mm. 14, 18 – Use a flexible wrist for string crossings. (See Practice Guide for Vivaldi etude-caprice, Section 1/F.)

m. 16 – Gradually come off the string for the spiccato. (On open strings, practice varying lengths of spiccatos as well as blending from detaché to spiccato.)

m. 19 – The appoggiatura B-natural should be on the beat. Trill for the full value of the dotted quarter, finishing with the two sixteenth notes at the end of the slur. Complete the phrase on the third beat with a little breath after the G.

Section 3

mm. 19 (middle), 20, 21, 23 – In the lower 3rd of the bow, use a somewhat marked spiccato for the three repeated D's at the beginning of this ominous new section and at the end of m. 21. Keep the vibrato going, though, to prevent separated notes from sounding too dry. Give them a lot of direction by gradually increasing the amount of bow on each note. Build suspense through the crescendo to m. 24.

m. 22 – Play these sixteenth notes on the string, opening up the detachés with the crescendo implied by the ascending line.

m. 25 – Drop down to a mysterious mezzo piano before the long crescendo to forte in m. 28.

mm. 29, 30 – Do not play through the sixteenth rests! But do keep the vibrato going even when the bow comes slightly off the string just after each sixteenth note. Build tension into m. 30, and explode into the restatement of the first theme.

m. 30 – Play all three notes of the D major chord at once, by whipping the up bow. Practice "whipping" the upbow on a single open string first. To do this, take the bow off the string at the end of a down bow. Keeping it in motion, drop at the point and push the up bow with a small burst of speed. A flexible bow hand is essential. Getting all three notes of the chord to sound at once on the up bow will feel a bit like a scoop, as part of an upward, clockwise arc will be described. Although the bow direction will be slightly "in," take care not to play too close to the bridge. Keep the fingers flexible, and in this etude-caprice, lead to the next chord. Keeping the bow in motion, practice the chords over and over, first individually, and then one after the other. (Open string equivalents and Appendix VI will be helpful if needed.)

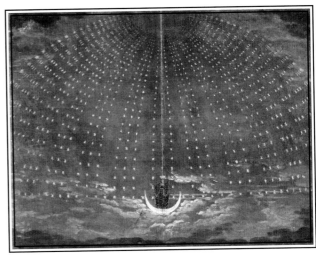

Stage set by Karl Friedrich Schinkel for the arrival of the Queen of the Night in an 1815 production of Mozart's opera, The Magic Flute.

Section 4

m. 31 – Establish the energy of the first theme once again with a vibrant tone, an exciting vibrato, and lots of direction!

m. 32 – As in m. 2, lift slightly between the two D's for the elegance of this style. Get back in the string again for the following two-note slur. Remember to keep a loose elbow for the two separate sixteenth notes (A and G) at the end of the measure.

m. 34 – Loosen the elbow for the two detaché notes after the slur in this measure as well, and again, keep the vibrato going while taking the bow off the string for the rest.

mm. 35, 36 – Vary the lengths of the spiccatos to accommodate the suggested dynamics. Blend from spiccato to detaché at the end of m. 36.

m. 37 – The sudden piano will be aided by a sounding point change at the end of the previous note (E). This should take the bow farther away from the bridge.

m. 38 – Spring the detachés with the slightest squeeze of the index finger on the bow. Broaden the lengths of these slightly separated sixteenth notes to crescendo into m. 39.

A portrait of Mozart's mother hangs on the wall behind the Mozart family in this painting of 1780-81 by Johann Nepomuk de la Croce.

m. 39 – A wide half step will help the intonation between the B-flat and A, and is especially important when repeating the same finger for the shift. Practice in slow motion first, with stops. (See Appendix II.) Lighten the 2nd finger, and pull with the whole arm easily down to 2nd position. Put the finger back down with the same amount of weight as it had to begin with.

m. 39 and 40 – Lean slightly on the appoggiatura, and end the trill by leading the two sixteenth notes to the last chord. Like the follow through of a golf swing, keep the bow moving throughout the chord and continue this motion while taking the bow off the strings. Remember to vibrate after the bow comes off the string to keep the sound ringing for as long as possible.

6. In the Style of Beethoven

Amy Barlowe

IN THE STYLE OF
Beethoven

 TECHNICAL ELEMENTS

Broken thirds
Arpeggios
Chromatics
2-step shifts
Finger extensions

 MUSICAL FEATURES

Dramatic dynamic changes
Sturm und Drang influence
Thematic contrast
Vibrato

PRACTICE GUIDE

Section 1

Ⓐ A loose elbow and flat bow hair will produce the cleanest and most open sounding detaché for all of the sixteenth notes in this section. Bounce fingers of the left hand for clear articulation.

Ⓑ **mm. 1 through 4** – Bring out the melodic notes with a slightly faster bow speed and a little more vibrato. Thinking polyphonically, notice how these melodic notes appear in the bass voice in mm. 1 and 3, while in mm. 2 and 4, they are in the soprano voice. Following the line for dynamics will help to bring out this alternation while highlighting the stormy, turbulent nature of the sixteenth note patterns.

Ⓒ **mm. 2 and 4** – Half moon symbols above or below fingerings, such as those found above the "4" for the C on beat three of m. 2 and below the "1" for the G-sharp at the end of m. 4, indicate extensions and contractions of fingers while remaining in a position. When placed above a finger number, an upward extension is indicated. When placed below a finger number, the finger must be pulled back. In the case of the C, the 4th finger will be extended; in the case of the G-sharp, the 1st finger will be pulled back.

Ⓓ Use a variety of rhythms to practice the sixteenth note passagework. (See Appendix IV.) Also try slurring passages (such as those in this section) that are originally written to be played separately. Articulation and rhythmic reversals are useful practice tools. They keep the mind alert and develop coordination, concentration and security.

Section 2

A   **mm. 5, 7** – Make the upper notes of each pair of sixteenths in these patterns more important than the lower notes by using a little more bow and vibrato. This should promote a noticeable sense of direction and enable the arpeggios to launch into the repeated E's. Continue to drive these E's forward by broadening a spiccato that starts at the balance of the bow, working towards the frog, and coming off the string more before the accented downbeat of m. 8.

B   **m. 6** – Drop and pull the accented F with passion. A faster, wider vibrato will add to the strength of the dotted quarter note, after which the energy can wane with the decrescendo to allow more strength to be gathered for the next upsurge in m. 7. From the 4th finger F to the 1st finger B, the hand will need to crawl back to 4th position via a two-step shift. Pull back the 3rd finger to play the D; then pivot slightly towards the scroll, allowing the thumb and 1st finger to gradually move into their new position before the shift to the G-sharp on the third beat of the measure.

C   **m. 8** – The decrescendo in this measure will effectively set up the change of character at the beginning of Section 3. Separate slightly the two eighth notes at the end of the measure.

Section 3

A   **m. 9** – Practice without the ornament first until the intonation and rhythm of the measure are secure. Then extract the A to the C (still without the turn). Play them by themselves; then play them by themselves again, but internally hear where the ornament will elegantly fit. Finally, play the first two notes with the ornament, allowing it to lead to the dotted quarter C. (Use this technique for all subsequent ornaments.)

B   The dark, expressive nature of this section reflects the tendency of the Sturm und Drang (Storm and Stress) movement to foreshadow the passion and intensity of the upcoming Romantic period.

C   **m. 9 through the middle of m. 12** – Try a whispered sotto voce (under voice) approach that will contribute to the desired sense of restlessness. A narrower and faster vibrato would be effective as well.

D   **m. 12** – Lighten after the 2nd eighth note (C). With a very small lift, take a slight breath between the two C's. Be careful not to over hold the tie.

E   **mm. 13, 14** – The crescendo of the previous measure should serve to open the emotional floodgates in these two measures. Use the bow freely, and widen the vibrato to make it stronger and more expressive.

F   **m. 15** – Use the descending chromatic scale to convey increasing sorrow. Keep the half steps wide. Practice with stops between each note to focus on intonation. (See Appendix II.)

G   **m. 16** – Crescendos to piano are quite common in the writing of Beethoven. The slightest slowing and the tiniest breath before the piano will give the sudden dynamic change more drama. Open the bow to crescendo during this moment of increasing optimism.

Beethoven-Haus: Beethoven's birthplace, now a museum in Bonn, Germany.

Section 4

A **m. 17** – Retake the bow with curved fingers, keeping springs in the hand for the second down bow E of the measure. This energy in the piano dynamic creates an emotional intensity. Treat the thirty-second notes as ornaments, propelling the measure towards the next down beat.

B **m. 19** – Keep a loose elbow for the detachés that occur between slurs. The two eighth notes at the end of the measure are portato. The slightest squeeze of the index finger in the context of the slur should accomplish this stroke. The bow should not stop, and keeping the left hand active with vibrato should prevent dryness in the sound.

C **mm. 21, 22** – Follow the line with dynamics. Make a dramatic crescendo to piano as in m. 16. This time, however, the line will continue to ascend as in a last effort to reach out before suffering resignation.

D **m. 23** – Once again, use the turns to energetically point the way to the end of the phrase. Keep the vibrato going as the bow is taken off the string for the rest.

Section 5

A The struggle begins again with the return of the A section. Give the sixteenth notes even more energy this time. Keep the bow hair flat. Loosen the elbow. Exaggerate everything suggested for the opening of the etude-caprice. Keep the left hand active with vibrato, and determine a sounding point appropriate to the energetic, fortissimo detaché bow strokes.

Lithograph from a journal of 1834 depicting Beethoven composing the Pastoral Symphony.

Franz Stober's watercolor painting of Beethoven's funeral procession, March 29, 1827.

Section 6

A **mm. 29, 30** – Exaggerate the dynamics and articulations of these measures to show even more direction.

B **mm. 31, 32** – Bring out the harmonic changes and open up the bow in the upper half as the ascending sequences herald the arrival of a triumphant ending.

C **mm. 33, 34, 35** – Retake the bow, curving the fingers before pulling. Show resolve by emphasizing the 2nd beat with a strong vibrato, a little extra weight, and bow speed. Punctuate the last arpeggiated polyphonic figure with sforzandos, and use sounding points to help sustain the sound on the subsequent slurs. Loosen elbow for the two detaché sixteenth notes at the end of the m. 35.

D **mm. 36, 37** – Lean on the appoggiatura to start the trill in the penultimate measure. Use the nachschlag to lead to the 3rd beat, but do not play this beat too heavily because it functions as a springboard to the chord preceding the last downbeat. Finish with solidity, pulling all three notes of the chord at once with relaxed fingers. (See Appendix VI.) Circle around for the last A, relaxing and then curving the fingers on the bow when approaching the string. Follow through, keeping the bow in motion and the left hand active with vibrato to end with resonance and zest!

Detail from *THE OATH OF THE HORATII*
Jacques-Louis David (1784–1785)

7. In the Style of Paganini

Amy Barlowe

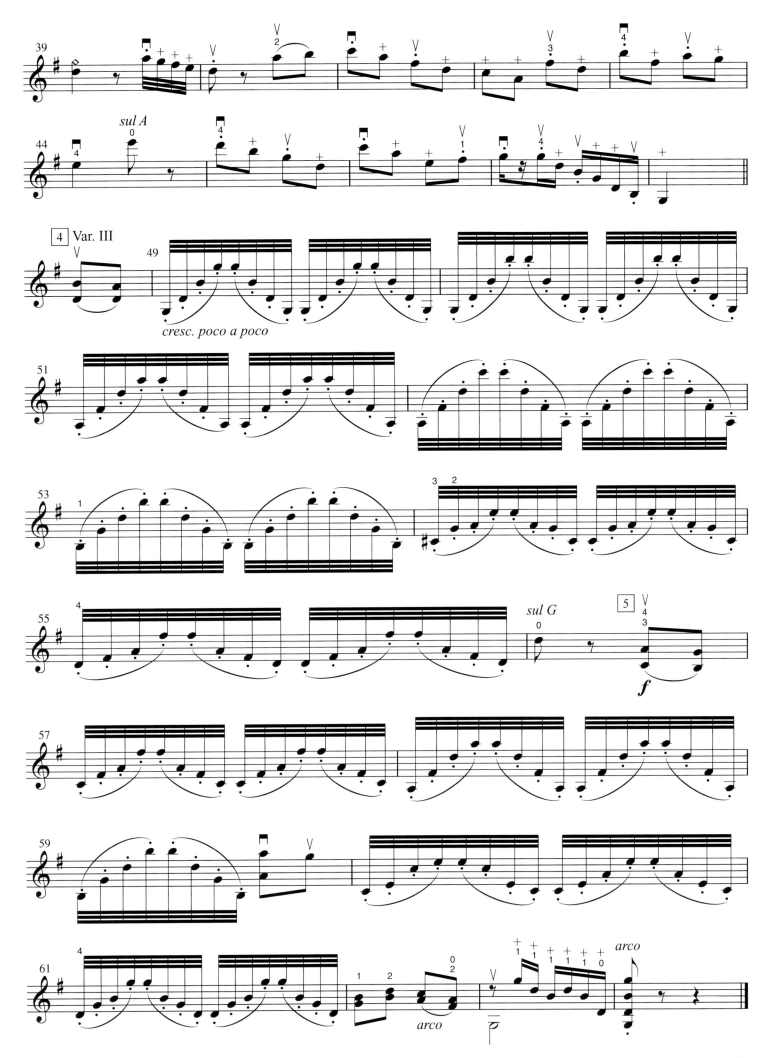

IN THE STYLE OF
Paganini

 TECHNICAL FEATURES

Flying spiccato
Left hand pizzicato
Harmonics
Ricochet

 MUSICAL FEATURES

Singing line
Phrasing
Virtuosic flair

PRACTICE GUIDE

Section 1

A This etude-caprice, a theme and variations, opens with a cantabile melody that requires a relaxed bow hand, an expressive bow, a loose elbow and a warm vibrato. Make bow changes inaudible, and keep the vibrato going.

B m. 1 – Connect the pick up to the downbeat of this measure with a smooth bow change and vibrato. When changing the bow, be sure to change on the same amount of hair. Prepare and time the shift to the D. Lighten the dot of the dotted eighth and sixteenth rhythm, and just slightly hop the bow to the F-sharp. Keep the vibrato going to prevent dryness, and lead the F-sharp to the down beat of m. 2.

C m. 3 – Changing the shape of the 2nd finger from the slightly extended C-sharp to the squared C-natural will widen the half step and help to secure the intonation.

D m. 14 – For harmonics to sound well, play as firmly with the bow as would be necessary for a solidly fingered note. Only the finger that is playing the harmonic should be lightened.

E mm. 15, 16 – End the theme with a charming sense of aplomb.

Section 2

A The dotted rhythm that begins the first variation can be somewhat over-dotted to create more contrast with the upcoming triplets. When shifting to 2nd position with the 1st finger (from B to C), lift this finger the slightest bit while remaining on the string. Be sure to shift with the thumb and whole arm as well. Then, put the first finger down once again, more firmly for the C. While making the shift, lighten the finger, not the bow. Lead to the downbeat of m. 17.

B mm. 17, 19, 25 – The grace notes at the beginnings of these measures need to feel almost like left hand pizzicatos as the fingers briefly touch the string before the main notes.

C The triplets with slurs and dots in this section are to be played as flying spiccatos. Using approximately the middle third of the bow, start the up bows where the detaché down bows finish. Start the first spiccato from the string, tossing the remaining four with the fingers and forearm. In this particular type of flying spiccato, allow the bow to travel towards the lower half, rather than recovering.

D mm. 20, 28 – Bring out the duples in the second halves of these measures, not unlike a sardonic gesture, before returning to the elegance of the flying spiccato triplet figures.

E mm. 23, 31 – Toss off these arpeggios with abandon. Vibrate the arrival notes of the following measures.

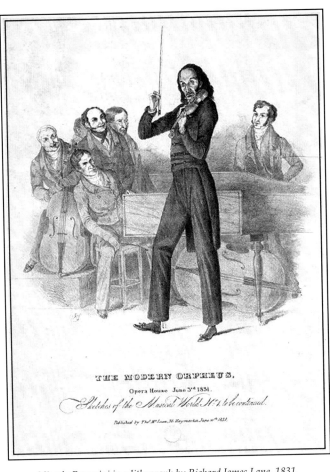

Niccolo Paganini in a lithograph by Richard James Lane, 1831.

Section 3

A The second variation employs left hand pizzicato and harmonics. Virtuosic techniques like these, although sometimes challenging to acquire, need to be practiced with patience until they can appear effortless.

B For the left hand pizzicato in this section, move the elbow slightly to the left to enable the fleshiest part of the finger to contact the string. Be sure to firmly place the finger responsible for the note to be sounded in order to get the best sound. Pluck into the palm of the hand.

C The bowed notes in measures with left hand pizzicato, such as those in m. 33, can be made to sound like pizzicato notes by dropping the bow more vertically in the upper half towards the point.

D The weight of the bow is critical for the playing of both artificial and natural harmonics. Although the finger is lightened to play harmonics, bilateral independence is required so that the weight of the bow remains the same as it would for solid notes. In addition, with artificial harmonics, it is essential that the lower finger is placed accurately and firmly to achieve the best results. (The dots with dashes above indicate an articulation that is separate but not too short.)

E m. 44 – Without altering the weight of the bow, gradually lighten the 4th finger, extending and eventually flattening its tip to facilitate the slide to the harmonic E on the A string.

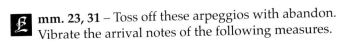

Section 4

A gift from a wealthy businessman, this violin was made by Joseph Guarnerius del Gesù in 1743. Paganini lovingly referred to it as "my cannon violin" because of its "explosive" sound. For this reason, it has come to be known as "Il Cannone".

A The third variation consists primarily of ricochet bowings. Considered an "uncontrolled" bowing, ricochet is dissimilar to the flying spiccato of Variation I in that it depends on the bow's natural bounce rather than the individual toss of each flying spiccato note. Ricochets work most easily in the upper middle of the bow. Arpeggios across four strings, such as those in Section 4, actually make ricochet easy to accomplish since the strings themselves can be used to propel the bow from one to the next. Keeping the hair flat with the stick directly above, give a slight vertical motion of the hand and fingers. This little flick will create the impulse needed to get the ricochet started on the lowest notes of the arpeggios and can be used on the highest notes as needed. Change strings with the whole arm, and keep the bow moving. As the practice tempo increases, the arm will prescribe a smooth arc. The analogy of a pendulum swing can also be helpful.

B m. 56 – Play the D harmonic on the G string with a light finger and a firm bow. (Bring the arm around to shift.)

Section 5

A (See Appendix V for double stop tips.)

B m. 63 – While sustaining the G, pluck the sixteenth notes in this measure with the 3rd finger of the left hand. In order to balance the sound so that the moving notes can be heard, pluck strongly with the left hand, and play less on the sustained open G.

C m. 64 – From the air and with flexible fingers, break the last chord quickly. Pull the sound well not too close to the bridge, starting the chord with the upper arm (shoulder down). Follow through with the whole arm, and vibrate as long as the sound is ringing in the air.

THEATRE ROYAL, COVENT GARDEN.

The Nobility, Gentry, and the Public, are respectfully informed that arrangements have been made with

SIGNOR PAGANINI,

For a Series of Four Concerts;

THE FIRST OF WHICH WILL TAKE PLACE ON

FRIDAY, JULY 6, 1832,

When will be performed some of his

FAVOURITE PIECES.

PART I.

GRAND SINFONIA. — — — — .Mozart.
BALLAD, Mr. WILSON.
CAVATINA, Signora PIETRALIA, "Ah! s'estinta." (Donna Caratia) Mercadante.

Grand Concerto,
ALLEGRO MAESTOSO,
Composed and performed by Signor PAGANINI.

AIR, Miss SHIRREFF, "The Soldier tired." (Trumpet obligato, Mr. E. Harper) Arne.

PART II.

GRAND OVERTURE to Der Freyschütz. — — C. M. von Weber.

The celebrated Sonata (on the Prayer in Pietro L'Eremita, followed by a Tema with Variations) composed and performed on ONE STRING ONLY, (the Fourth String,) by **SIGNOR PAGANINI.**

DUET, Mr. WILSON and Mr. MORLEY, "Love and War." T. Cooke.
BALLAD Miss SHIRREFF, T. Welsh.

Variations on the Country Dance, Delle Streghe alla noce di Benevento, (or the Comic Dance of the Witches under the Walnut Tree of Benevento,) composed and performed by **SIGNOR PAGANINI,**

Leader of the Band, Mr. WODARCH,
Conductor, — SIR GEORGE SMART.

Announcement of the first of Paganini's four performances in Covent Garden, as always including many of the composer's own works.

8. In the Style of Brahms

Amy Barlowe

IN THE STYLE OF
Brahms

TECHNICAL FEATURES

Duplets vs. Triplets
Chords
Off string bowings
Sounding points

MUSICAL FEATURES

Long lines
Vibrato
Character
Sound

PRACTICE GUIDE

Section 1

A **m. 1** – Practice the intervals of both chords in double stops until they are dependably in tune vertically within each chord. Then practice back and forth between both chords to feel the finger relationships created horizontally. Only the 1st finger is moving, simplifying the process. (See Appendix VI.) When the chords are learned well, with broad bows, pure intonation and a strong vibrato, show direction by going to the 3rd beat of this measure. Brahms' lines are long. Fill them with a sense of restlessness, characterizing this passionate etude-caprice. Retake the bow for the eighth note D at the end of the measure. For the line to extend, keep the sound spinning from the previous chord with plenty of vibrato. Do not let the vibrato stop while retaking and playing the pick up to the next measure.

B **m. 2** – Enjoy the richness and depth of the G string. When shifting upwards on this string, play with a slower bow. Expect the sounding point to be close to the bridge. (See Appendix III.) Feel two against three when playing the duplet and triplet at the beginning of this measure and all similar figures throughout the etude-caprice. Without playing, subdivide and count aloud to a slow beat on a metronome, "1-2, 1-2-3." The duple will most likely be a little broader than expected. The triplet must be even. Lift the A slightly before the hooked D at the end of the measure. Draw the line out further by continuing the sound with vibrato. Lead to the down beat of the next measure.

C **m. 3** – Give a little more direction towards the 3rd beat with vibrato and energy. Remember to keep the fingers flexible. Circle around before the chord, keeping the bow in motion at the approach of the strings. Pull in with the upper arm to start the chords. (See Appendix VI.)

D **m. 4** – Give the eighth note rest at the end of the measure electricity. Follow the line with dynamics, and crescendo to the top D, keeping the vibrato going as the bow comes off the string.

Section 2

A **m. 5** – Sing the poco forte with passion, using a warm romantic vibrato. Loosen the joints of the fingers, and play a little more on their pads, rolling well. Be careful not to vibrate above the pitch because the tendency is to sound sharp.

B **m. 6** – Differentiate between dotted rhythms and triplets. (Hint: Practice counting aloud, "1-e-and-a, trip-o-let" to the pulse of this etude-caprice until the subdivisions are accurate and quite comfortable back to back.)

C **m. 7** – Be sure to notice the significant differences in note values between this measure and m. 6. Count carefully.

D **mm. 8, 9** – Use the left hand, bow speed and sounding point to create slight swells as the line sinks. Continue to extend the line with direction.

Brahms was born in this house in Hamburg. He and his family lived on the left hand side of the first floor, behind the double windows. The photograph was taken in 1891.

Section 3

A **m. 10** – Retake to start with an up bow. Broaden the spiccato in the lower part of the bow to crescendo. Arrive on the G with a strong vibrato. Hold the sound with a slow bow closer to the bridge. (Playing the music of Brahms requires strong 4th fingers. Practice 4th finger scales to strengthen this commonly weaker finger.)

B **mm. 11, 12, 13, 14** – Come off of the tie precisely in m. 11. Use plenty of bow to start the two-note slurs, reducing proportionally towards the middle with the decrescendo. Be careful not to slow down in the process. Detach the last sixteenth note of m. 13, but vibrate and lead to the long D of the next measure. Observe the swell from the 2nd beat of m. 13 into m. 14. As the tension momentarily subsides, allow the long line to phrase off before restlessness returns, growing into the next passionate expression.

Section 4

A **mm. 15, 16** – Keeping these two measures soft, will add to the underlying agitation. If intonation is a problem in m. 16, take the triplet on the 3rd beat out of context and, along with the F-sharp of the next duplet, practice the three double stops that can be derived from this combination. (See Appendix V.)

B **mm. 17, 18** – Sing m. 17 warmly, but with less intensity than the earlier gesture an octave above. Briefly release the tension built up in the previous measures. Catch the line as it fights resignation by intensifying the vibrato on the crescendo of m. 18, and by swirling dramatically from the thirty-second notes into the triplet of m. 19.

Section 5

A The forte triplet should launch the return of the first theme. As much as possible, connect the triplet to the ensuing chord. Keep the line long and the sound rich. Once again, be sure to differentiate the triplets from the dotted eighths and sixteenths. Capture the agitated spirit with a faster, narrower vibrato, energy and direction.

Section 6

A **mm. 23, 24** – Use a flexible wrist and play these soft triplets closer to the fingerboard, giving them a sweet tranquility amidst the turmoil of the surrounding material. Secure the intonation with the use of double stops and rhythms. When dependable, add a touch of vibrato.

B **mm. 25, 26, 27** – Use the eighth rests to give a sense of urgency as the next two measures build to the passionate climax of the etude-caprice. Accentuate, only slightly, the syncopation in m. 26. Keep the vibrato going on the C just prior to the electrical eighth rest of m. 27.

C **m. 28** – Release the energy and momentum built in the previous three measures by dropping and pulling the E-flat at the beginning of this measure with a bow speed that is not too fast. Use a strong vibrato, plenty of bow, and a loose elbow to let this measure freely sing with great warmth and emotion.

D **mm. 29, 30** – Further extend the line through these two measures, with yearning swells, lessening as the line drops. Ease the tempo with subtlety just towards the end of m. 30, at the bottom of the diminuendo.

Brahms in an uncommonly relaxed pose as he sits in a garden chair, cigar in hand.

Section 7

A **mm. 37, 38** – Briefly hold back the tempo, but keep the integrity of the duplet-triplet relationship while making the crescendo to the end of the line. Count very carefully the dotted quarter and eighth on the 3rd beat of m. 38.

B **mm. 39, 40** – Sustain the E-flat of m. 39 with a strong vibrato. Lighten the faster up bow D leading to the down beat of m. 40. When the intonation of the C minor chord on the 3rd beat of m. 40 is dependable, give it plenty of resonance by pulling all three notes at once and vibrating strongly. (See Appendix VI.)

C **m. 40** – Take the slightest bit of time to poise the whole note C before dropping and pulling it with a rich sound and strong vibrato.

* When this etude-caprice has been mastered as written, feeling it in a broad two beats per measure will allow it to flow more musically.

Detail from *THE POND*
Paul Cézanne (1876)

9. In the Style of Sarasate

Amy Barlowe

IN THE STYLE OF
Sarasate

TECHNICAL FEATURES

Flying spiccato
Harmonics
Left hand pizzicato
Octaves

MUSICAL FEATURES

Spanish flavor
Gypsy style
Rubato

PRACTICE GUIDE

Section 1

A   **m. 1** – Pluck the chord with gypsy bravura in an upward arc. Vibrate to give more resonance.

B   **m. 2, 3** – Rubato is a flexibility literally meaning "stolen time." In this case, a rubato with a Spanish flavor might consist of the following: a) with a rich, dark sound, begin m. 2 a little slower, taking a little extra time getting from the A to the B-flat; b) move the B-flat and C forward to the D; c) slightly slow the D to the C; d) take the tiniest breath and lift before the triplet of m. 3; e) drop, and vibrating the B-flat momentarily for emphasis, move the triplet in typically Spanish fashion quickly to the A. The key to rubato playing is subtlety. *Practice rubatos by hearing them in the mind's ear first. Develop a sound image.* Then play this image. Repeat this process (hear and play) over and over until the image is matched as closely as possible. Listen to a wide variety of Spanish gypsy music to become familiar with the style.

C   Cadenzas originated in improvisation. Singers would often perform short cadenzas in one breath. When performing cadenzas, give the impression that they are being composed spontaneously.

D   **m. 4** – Practice the series of A major arpeggiated figures in separate bows, martelé, rhythms and varying numbers of slurs in and out of rhythms. (See Appendix IV.) It is vital that every note be played with accuracy and clarity. Build each individual gesture until it is reliable. Then, because this cadenza is, in effect, a written out rubato, hear it inside first. The overall impression will be one of going to the top A with virtuosic flair, but subtleties at the beginning and end are encouraged. For example, start a little slower by adding a touch of vibrato to the low A before moving. Expand the slightest bit before the fermata. These are two flexibilities that would make a performance more natural and exciting.

m. 5 – Once again, pluck this chord in a sweeping arc. This time, pluck it with a sense of completion and authority. Let it ring with vibrato.

Section 2

The slurred eighth notes with dots in this etude-caprice are to be played as flying spiccatos. (See Practice Guide for Paganini – 2/C.)

m. 6 – As though it were a long pick up, give direction to these five eighth notes, pointing them towards the down beat of m. 7. Crescendo to follow the line as well. (Hint: Keep the bow hand loose!)

mm. 7, 8 – Tossed in the previous measure of flying spiccatos, the bow should land with elegance on the second beat of m. 7. Toss the eighth note D at the end of m. 7 to the A on the downbeat of m. 8 and on to the second beat as well. Continue on in this fashion tossing easily as in a good volley. Keeping the bow moving, rely on the resiliency of the stick and springs in the hand to do the work. In keeping with the nature of this etude-caprice, strive to make all of these gestures sound and appear effortless.

Sarasate studied at the Paris Conservatory when he was 12 years old. At 17, he won the conservatory's highest honor, the Premier Prix. (Photographed by Andreas Praefcke.)

The grace notes in this etude-caprice are to be played quickly and accurately before the beat.

mm. 14, 15, 16 – Use a broad spiccato below the middle of the bow for the harmonics in these measures. Direct them towards the down beat of every subsequent measure.

m. 17 – Do not use too much bow on the slur. (See Appendix III for sounding points.) Pull the slightest bit in (towards the bridge) with the hand. When finished with the slur, the bow will be on the sounding point for the spiccatos where it can straighten and get ready for the slower and longer detaché stroke.

m. 18 – Retake for the down bow slur. (Think horizontally while approaching the string.) Landing on springs, get back into the string with a warm sound before making the diminuendo to m. 19. Loosen the elbow for the detaché at the end of the measure.

mm. 21, 22 – Practice back and forth between an artificial harmonic and a natural harmonic. Artificial harmonics require the lower finger to be held down rather firmly while the upper finger is played lightly. Natural harmonics call for one finger to be lightened. Do not change the weight of the bow when playing them in succession. (See Practice Guide for Paganini – 3/D.) End the section by playing pure harmonics in a broad spiccato, conveying a gypsy's sense of assured optimism.

Section 3

mm. 23, 24 – (See Practice Guide for Paganini for tips on left hand pizzicato – 3/A, B and C.)

m. 25 – Get back into the string for the slur, and take a light up bow for the open E at the end of the measure. The trill should start from the note.

m. 30 – Use a slightly broader spiccato here, and show direction.

mm. 31, 32 – The slightest flick of the wrist will enable the quick string crossings in these two measures to be done with ease. But practice them slowly at first, exaggerating the appropriate motions of the wrist for the strings being crossed. (See Practice guide for Vivaldi – 1/F.)

m. 34 – The separate bows in this measure can start on the string as detaché and gradually blend into the broad spiccato to be used for the octaves that follow.

mm. 35, 36 – Practice these octaves individually first, until they sound like one note. The shape of the hand should be in its most natural frame, the fourth finger being curved. When every octave is able to be played in tune by itself, practice back and forth between two different octaves. (There is no need to play all three of the same octave for this type of practice.) Release the fingers and bring the arm around to shift. Lead with the first finger. (See Appendix V for double stop practice techniques.) Make all shifts elegant without jerking. Time them at the slower speeds, then build proportionally. After shifting with the thumb and whole arm, be sure to put the fingers back down firmly enough. When two octaves in succession remain in tune at least three times in a row, add another. Continue with this procedure until all octaves are in tune when played successively. Then practice as written, slowly at first and building when ready.

mm. 37, 38 – Pluck strongly!

While waiting for plans to work out in Sir Arthur Conan Doyle's, Red Headed League, *Sherlock Holmes and Dr. Watson decide to attend a concert by Sarasate who often performed in London.*

Section 4

m. 38 – Play the thirty-second notes at the end of the measure accurately. With the diminuendo, allow them to flow back into the suavity and graciousness of the first theme.

mm. 46, 47, 48 – These three measures require a flexible wrist and pure intonation. Use a relaxed, but firm bow for the harmonics.

m. 49 – Take the bow off the string after the G, and let it bounce for the next two spiccatos before landing with elegance on the tie. (Count the tie accurately.)

m. 56 – (See earlier comments on the practice and playing of cadenzas.) Use the sounding point for the G string to help keep a rich, clear tone while ascending the string. Also keep in mind that the higher up the finger is placed, the closer to the bridge will be the sounding point. Because of the speed of the last arpeggio, it would be helpful to have one or two landmarks within the passage. In that way, the last flourish can be played with gypsy abandon.

Pluck the last chord in a flamboyant upward arc. Vibrate as long as the sound remains in the air. Perform this gesture with the utmost panache!

Note: Warm the sound of this etude-caprice (much like a romantic salon piece) with a vibrato aided by a loose first joint that facilitates covering plenty of finger when rolled.

10. In the Style of Ravel

Amy Barlowe

IN THE STYLE OF
Ravel

 TECHNICAL FEATURES

Legato bow stroke
Sounding points
Changing meters
Harmonics

 MUSICAL FEATURES

French sound
Variety in repetitions
Colors

PRACTICE GUIDE

Section 1

A There are many commonalities between the paintings of French Impressionist painter, Claude Monet, and the compositions of Maurice Ravel. Hazy, luminous images, many of water scenes or landscapes, find their counterparts in flowing, metrically varied melodies, muted colors, and a typically French sound that mirrors the language.

B Impressionist painters viewed and painted subject matter in differing lighting conditions. Because music is temporal, repetition is often used to reinforce a gesture in the listener's ear. No one, however, enjoys being told the same thing twice in the same way. Be imaginative, but subtle when varying the repetitions in the opening measures and throughout this etude-caprice.

C Considering the sound of the French language, add fluidity to bow changes and strokes, and use colorful sounding points. Adopt a vibrato that is narrower and slightly faster to give this etude-caprice even more of a French sound.

D A legato left hand adds more fluidity to bowed legato. Keep fingers close to the strings, placing them without force or great speed.

E **mm. 3, 4** – By contrast to the first two rather lazy measures, show direction in m. 3 by pointing the repeated figure towards the end of the phrase at m. 4. The most subtle forward movement and crescendo will be enough to be effective.

ℰ **mm. 5, 6, 7, 8** - Keep the vibrato going for the harmonics, and approach them with a firm, but relaxed bow. Reflect the first phrase, but give this phrase more direction and resolve.

Section 2

Ⓐ With a little more motion, play the thirty-second note arpeggios on the fingerboard for a color contrast. Keep the bow moving and the fingers down as the arm swings in arcs.

Ⓑ **m. 10** – Maintaining approximately the same intervallic distances between fingers, lighten them just enough to shift up a half step before putting them down again. Move the hand (with thumb) and whole arm up as a unit. Use double stops to help secure the intonation on both arpeggios.

Maurice Ravel at the piano, 1912.

Leon Bakst set design for Act II of Ravel's ballet, Daphnis and Chloe

Ⓒ The eighth note remains the same for all of the meter changes throughout this etude-caprice.

Ⓓ **m. 11**– This section ends with a wash of color. The sudden dynamic change will require a new sounding point that is somewhat closer to the bridge. Having kept fingers down, the A-sharp that begins this measure should already be there. Take the slurs out for practice, and use rhythms for added dependability. (See Appendix IV.)

Section 3

Ⓐ **mm. 12, 13** – With a warm sound, gradually broaden these two measures, feeling them in an expanding two. Follow the line for dynamics.

Ⓑ **m. 13** – Crescendo while the notes descend in the second half of the measure, creating tension in the contradiction.

Ⓒ **m. 14** – Play this 3/8 measure with tender softness and reluctance, intentionally giving a rather tentative start to the more animated 6/8.

ⓓ mm. 17, 18 – Allow the repetitions to accumulate and pour into another wash of color. Be sure to be able to subdivide this measure accurately before playing it in two sweeping beats. Removing the slurs and practicing in rhythms will solidify the intervallic relationships eventually enabling the measure to easily flow. (See Appendix IV.)

ⓔ mm. 19, 21 – Warm the sound with vibrato, but keep the French sound in mind. Let the sixteenth-note pairs transport each gesture to the next. Follow the line dynamically, within each measure as well as sequentially. Darken the color with a little less bow and bow speed at m. 21.

ⓕ mm. 20, 22 – Brighten these somewhat more optimistic measures with attention to rhythmic precision. Give the sixteenth notes in these two measures a dance-like swirl to the next beat. (The figure "eighth, dotted eighth, sixteenth" is reminiscent of the opening motive, but is more animated in this context.) Without a distinct accent, very slightly detach the last A in m. 22. Keep the vibrato active to avoid dryness.

The Houses of Parliament (Palace of Westminster) in one of a series of paintings by Claude Monet (1840-1926), painted in different weather conditions and at various times of day. Ravel's impressionist compositions reflect the ephemeral qualities of Monet's paintings.

ⓖ mm. 23, 24, 25 – With a big crescendo on the A minor arpeggio of m. 23, sustain the sound using sounding points to advantage. Emphasize the last two eighth notes of m. 23 with a little more vibrato and a slight sink, and release on each note. Keep the bow moving in the context of a slur. Connect to m. 25 with vibrato and a legato bow change. Gradually ease into the return of the first theme.

Section 4

ⓐ mm. 26, 27, 28, 29 – Revisit the relaxed character of the opening, but with a little less innocence. Crescendo m. 29 more noticeably this time, pointing towards the top of the phrase, the harmonic E.

ⓑ mm. 32, 33 – Use the repetition for dynamic growth and reinforcement, leading to the three emphatically held back quarter notes of m. 33. With time, allow the sound of the last harmonic to be suspended in the air before proceeding to the last measure.

ⓒ m. 34 – Return to the original tempo and keep the vibrato going while plucking with the fleshy part of the finger in order to get the warmest pizzicato sound. Take a breath to poise the last harmonic. After holding the fermata approximately double the note value, drift off the sounding point, feathering the sound until it finally disappears.

Detail from *WESTMINSTER ABBEY*
Canaletto (1749)

11. In the Style of Bartók

Amy Barlowe

IN THE STYLE OF
Bartók

TECHNICAL ELEMENTS
Rhythm
Chords
Left hand pizzicato
Ornaments
Harmonics

MUSICAL ELEMENTS
Characteristics of Slovak folk music
Phrase direction
Dynamics
Articulation

PRACTICE GUIDE

Section 1

Ⓐ Bring out the rhythmic vitality of this etude-caprice with well planned articulations and careful attention to the rhythms and special effects. Once these details are set, remember that this etude-caprice is based on the ingredients of Hungarian folk music. To make it convincing, it needs to be colorful and vibrant. Use imagination and energy to bring it to life. Eventually, this etude-caprice should be played with abandon!

Ⓑ **mm. 1, 2** – Drop and pull the bow for the down beats, and whip the up bows for the accents (See Mozart etude-caprice, Section 3/E.) Play firmly with the bow on the harmonics to get the best sound. Use the 4th finger for double harmonics. While lightening the fingers to play harmonics, the weight of the bow on the strings should remain the same as it would be for notes that are not harmonics. Keep the bow moving.

Ⓒ **m. 3** – Three-note chords such as the one in this measure require flexibility in the fingers of the right hand. The fingers pull the chord along with the whole arm. (Reminder: Keep the shoulder down for a relaxed approach.) The three-note chords in this etude-caprice are not particularly difficult because they all have an open string on the bottom. In many instances, tuning the middle notes of the chords to the open strings an octave below will be a good way to start working on getting the whole chord in tune. Be sure the intonation of the top two notes is as perfect as possible before attempting three notes. (To practice the chords so that they sound their best, see Appendix VI.)

Count both voices carefully. (*Reminder: Dividing a beat into 2 parts in this meter, as in the pizzicato eighth notes, count "1 and 2 and." When dividing a beat into 4 parts, count "1 e and a." So, for a sixteenth note that is followed by a dotted eighth note, say "1" for the sixteenth and "e and a" for the dotted eighth note.*) Counting with syllables allows both voices to fit together easily and keeps rhythms precise so that a figure such as this one does not metamorphose into a triplet.

D m. 6 – Ornaments (grace notes) are decorations, so they should not sound as important as their main notes. Play the surrounding notes without ornaments first. Play them again, this time hearing where they should be. Then play ornaments as written.

E mm. 3, 5, 7 – Use a burst of bow speed for the accents.

F Reminder: Pluck towards the palm of the hand for left hand pizzicati.

G m. 9 – Sound the 4th finger A with the open A. Then drop the elbow to the A string level and pluck the D with the left hand.

THE BARTÓK CABIN

The cabin in Saranac Lake, New York, where Bartok wrote one of his last two works, the Viola Concerto. (Drawing by artist, James W. Hotaling, courtesy of Historic Saranac Lake.)

Section 2

A m. 13 – Count carefully. If necessary, count aloud playing only the top line. Then add the chords without disturbing the rhythm.

B m. 13, 15 – Play lightly on the sixteenth notes following the chords. Otherwise, their speed may make them sound too heavy or accented.

C mm. 14, 18 – Main notes need to arrive on the downbeats. The grace notes that come before these main notes should be tucked in between the measures anticipating the downbeats.

Section 3

A m. 19 – Start with an extended 4th finger on the E-flat. Pull back to a squared 4th finger on the D. Make the half step wide. Practice this measure in separate bows and rhythms for accurate intonation. Then put the slurs back. Use rhythms again with the slurs for accuracy. (See Appendix IV.)

B mm. 23 through 30 – Observe all articulation markings carefully. In this case, dots over notes at the ends of slurs will indicate a slight lift after the slur. The dot over the B-flat at m. 26 indicates a slight lift after the B-flat to separate it from the two slurred sixteenths that follow. The second G in m. 30 is to be articulated in the same way. Dashes above or below a note indicate an arrival or a little more length.

Section 4

A mm. 31 through m. 35 – The solid finger of an artificial harmonic must be firm, but do not squeeze the thumb. Pull the bow firmly and somewhat faster (away from bridge) to make these harmonics sound well. Practice one at a time in mm. 33 and 34, adding on as they become easier. Try playing them with both fingers solid first. The results will not be the notes that are meant to be sounded, but finger placement will be secure before lightening. In a series of these harmonics, release the hand between each one.

B m. 37 – This time, play the 4th finger A (on the D string) and open A string together, and raise the elbow to the D string level in order to pluck the open A on the 2nd beat with the left hand.

Section 5

A mm. 41, 42 – Dashes above eighth notes indicate slight separation and emphasis during the crescendo.

Section 6

A mm. 47 through 56 – Dots above or below eighth notes in this section indicate spiccato. In this case, lower in the bow and with flexible fingers, use the upper arm a little more to drop the bow on the string for a more marked and energetic spiccato. Let the bow do the work, and give this section lots of life! (Hint: Keep the shoulder down.)

This is the way the Budapest Opera House would have looked during Bartok's youth. Eventually, he would conduct here.

B m. 49 – Stay in 3rd position. Extend the 3rd finger from C-sharp to D. Bring it back to its original position on the C-sharp grace note before the downbeat of m. 50.

C m. 53 – Release the hand between each octave to decrease tension. Count accurately.

D m. 54 – Lift the bow after the second A octave to phrase. Keep the bow in motion before the spiccatos of the next measure.

Section 7

A mm. 63, 64 – Once again the dashes are for slight separation. Give the eighth notes in these two measures greater emphasis than before.

Czech peasants sing folk songs into a gramophone as Bartok records their music for reference.

B mm. 63, 64 – Prepare the shifts by coming around with the arm. (See Appendix II.) To practice the shifts in this scale pattern, also try the following: slide slowly from G to D on the 1st finger, bringing the arm around. Repeat until dependable. Extract a G major arpeggio from the scale pattern. Practice a glissando (sliding) arpeggio (G- B- D) with the 1st finger. Then practice G, B and D in martelé, slowly, without rhythm, until it is secure. Next practice these notes in detaché. Add notes in between, but feel the original arpeggio, still without rhythm. Add the rhythm. Add the remaining notes in m. 64. Be careful of the intonation between the E-flat and F-sharp. Be sure the step and a half is wide enough. Add the articulation. Add the crescendo.

C mm. 67, 68 – Whip the up bow to accent the natural harmonics on the second beat of m. 67. Come off the string in a slight arc and curve the fingers before dropping and pulling the last chord with finality. Let the sound ring as the bow comes off the strings with flair!

12. In the Style of Copland

Amy Barlowe

IN THE STYLE OF
Copland

TECHNICAL ELEMENTS

Octaves
Rhythmic angularity
Melodic angularity
Arpeggios
Quick scale passages

MUSICAL ELEMENTS

Purity of sound
Americana
Line
Imagination

PRACTICE GUIDE

Section 1

A Developing imagery would be a useful and creative way to approach this etude-caprice. Early American landscapes, and social affairs may be good points of departure.

B The thirty-second note scale passages in this etude-caprice require accuracy and agility. Violinists learn D and A Major scales early in their studies, so playing these scales quickly may seem like an easy task. Do not take them for granted, however. Performance can never be convincing when care has not been given to intonation. If notes blur or are prone to even slight intonation inaccuracies, take the passages out of their respective slurs, and use the stop bow method to target weak spots. (See Appendix II.) Once the intervallic relationships between fingers are dependable, use rhythms to build accuracy and coordination. When ready, try accumulations to build the speed. On an up bow, play the first note. Then go back and play the first and second notes as fast as possible then the first, second and third notes. Continue adding on until all notes are clean and in tune. (Note: Cure one problem at a time before approaching the octave. The octave will have its own problems. Getting to it consistently will pose yet another.)

C Finger bouncing is a great tool for building speed. Rather than pressing and holding down fingers in fast passagework, the sensation of tapping actually helps to relax the left hand.

D Once the quick scales are secure, add the crescendos and broaden their very ends almost imperceptibly to give more dramatic direction.

E m. 1 – Count this measure accurately. Connect the fast scale to the octave with the arm and flexible fingers. (When the octave is perfectly in tune, the two notes will sound like one.) If necessary, practice accumulations backwards, adding one note at a time and building speed to connect with the octave. (i.e., C to the octave D's; B to C to octave; A to B to C to octave, etc.) With a burst of vibrato and bow speed, pull the bow fast and then slower for the accent.

F m. 2 – Bring the arm around when shifting to the 5th position D that starts this measure. If necessary, practice replacing the 4th finger D with the 2nd finger D using the stop bow method. (See Appendix II.)

G mm. 2, 3 – In preparation for the accented up bow on the downbeat of m. 3, save the bow on the up bow slur at the end of m. 2.

H Articulate the syncopations in this etude-caprice to better communicate the folk-like displacement of the beat.

I mm. 3, 4 - Accent the short down beats of these measures to further reinforce the angularity of this rustic melody.

J mm. 5, 6 – Build the long crescendo with pure intonation on the arpeggios. Strengthen the vibrato on the A at the peak of the phrase by opening it with the crescendo. Let the A bloom.

K The quarter note will remain constant throughout all of the meter changes in this etude-caprice.

L mm. 7, 8 – Expand the last two beats of m. 7. Accent with bursts of bow speed. Take time to poise the accented D as a solid conclusion to this introductory opening.

Section 2

A mm. 9, 10 – Keeping the tempo of the opening, slightly separate the notes of these two measures from one another, being sure to balance well on both strings for the double stops. The soft dynamic and quaint nature of this dance-like section call for a rather classical vibrato, not too wide or too fast.

B mm. 11, 12 – Allow this melody to soar with a vibrato that widens at the peak of the crescendo.

C m. 13 – A nostalgic reminder of the introduction, these syncopations can move ahead with more warmth and a little less articulation than previously.

D mm. 15, 16, 17, 18 – Continue to play the separate notes slightly non legato. Add tempo flexibilities after intonation, rhythm and articulations are secure. Use imagination to bring these measures to life. For example, m. 18 could be a reflective moment, considering the nature of the previous measure. Use dynamics, bow speeds, sounding point changes, and vibrato for poignancy and color.

Section 3

A Open up the sound, and sing freely, organizing the bow throughout this section to maximize expressivity while keeping a good core to the sound. Employ sounding points and bow speeds for these purposes as well. Keep the bow moving with flexibility in the arm, wrist and fingers to give the sound freedom and openness.

B mm. 20, 21 – Guard against accents on notes of less importance when they fall on shorter note values than their successors. For example, the quarter note on the first beat of m. 20 will use a faster bow than the slurred dotted quarter and eighth. Play with slightly less bow speed and weight on the quarter note, and be a little heavier on the slur to compensate. (Holding the tip closer to the bridge by pulling out the hand very slightly on the note before and keeping it out for most of the duration of the slur will also help to bring out the more expressive dotted quarter note. See Appendix III.)

Aaron Copland at the piano at Rock Hill, his beloved home in Peekskill, NY (1978).

C Increasingly warm and round, faster with more width and strength at the forte, lessening at the diminuendo, vary the vibrato by mirroring the heartbeat in this section.

D m. 22 – The diminuendo and gradual slowing down of this measure serves to help dramatize the contrast between this section and the return of the opening material.

Section 4

A This time, appearing in the dominant key of A major, play this section with spirit and confidence. Use imagination to differentiate between this section and the opening. Some exaggeration of dynamics and articulations can be used for this purpose. To polish this section, review the practice techniques suggested for Section 1.

Aaron Copland gave master classes in the Tappan Manor House, which is on the grounds of Tanglewood in Lenox, Massachusetts. (Photo by Amy Barlowe.)

Aaron Copland with cat, ca. 1947 (Photo courtesy of Aaron Copland Fund.)

Section 5

A mm. 29, 30, 31, 32 – With a brief change of color, these fragments are once again nostalgic memories. Pull a pure sound on appropriate sounding points not too close to the bridge. Sweetly sing with a continuous vibrato as though trying to hold onto a vanishing dream.

B m. 33 – Conveying sincerity and conviction, make the last statement a proud flourish with the syncopations more accentuated for emphasis.

C m. 34 – Pull the chords with the whole arm and flexible fingers, sounding all three notes at once, the second chord slightly stronger than the first to show the direction. If the interval of the fifth is problematic when covering both strings, lean the 3rd finger slightly towards whichever string sounds flat. Vibrate the chords, and vibrate after taking the bow off of the strings to get the most resonance possible. (If needed, see Appendix VI for chord strategies.)

D m. 35 – Delay the last ascending scale just enough to make its last upward sweep even more assertive. Accent the octave D's away from the bridge. Pull in slightly with the hand to bring the bow closer to the bridge. Continue to hold the double forte octave on a slow bow that straightens by opening out approximately at the curve of the stick. Keep the vibrato going beyond the point where the bow is dramatically taken off the string. As long as there is sound spinning in the air, it should be vibrated.

CHRONOLOGICAL CORRELATIONS

DATES Composers	Artists	Writers/Philosophers	CONCURRENT EVENTS
(1678–1741) A. Vivaldi	(1659–1743) H. Rigaud	(1668–1744) G. Vico	(1701) Prince Eugene of Savoy (the Hapsburg general) invades Milan at the beginning of the War of the Spanish Succession.
(1685–1750) J.S. Bach	(1696–1770) G.B. Tiepolo	(1667–1745) J. Swift	(1688) William of Orange and Mary Stuart become rulers of the Parliament.
(1685–1759) G.F. Handel	(1697–1768) A. Canaletto	(1694–1778) Voltaire	(1707) Scotland and England are united, creating the Kingdom of Great Britain.
(1732–1809) J. Haydn	(1732–1806) J. Fragonard	(1724–1804) I. Kant	(Late 1700s–1815) The Napoleonic Wars are being fought.
(1756–1791) W.A. Mozart	(1755–1842) E. Vigée-Lebrun	(1749–1838) L. da Ponte	(1776) America's Declaration of Independence is signed.
(1770–1827) L. van Beethoven	(1746–1828) F. Goya	(1775–1817) J. Austen	(1789) The French Revolution begins.
(1782–1840) N. Paganini	(1748–1825) J. David	(1749–1832) J. Goethe	(1796) Napoleon's first Italian campaign takes place.
(1833–1897) J. Brahms	(1834–1903) J. Whistler	(1828–1906) H. Ibsen	(1839) Writings on the daguerreotype process are published revolutionizing photography.
(1844–1908) P. Sarasate	(1839–1906) P. Cezanne	(1844–1900) F. Nietzsche	(1874) The first exhibit of Impressionist art is held.
(1875–1937) M. Ravel	(1864–1901) Toulouse-Lautrec	(1871–1922) M. Proust	(1889) The Eiffel Tower is built.
(1881–1945) B. Bartok	(1882–1963) G. Braque	(1882–1941) J. Joyce	(1903) The Wright brothers begin The Age of Aviation.
(1900–1990) A. Copland	(1889–1975) T.H. Benton	(1905–1980) J.P. Sartre	(1939–1945) World War II is fought.

APPENDIX I

GENERAL PRACTICE HINTS

1. ALWAYS be alert enough to **THINK! Repetition** without **reason** is a waste of time!

2. Use **"inner speech"** to help be your own teacher.

3. Make friends with a **metronome**.

4. Practice **consistently**, on a daily basis, and work to develop patience. Set short and long term goals, and always have something to look forward to while practicing. The smallest accomplishment can be extremely gratifying if practice is approached positively.

5. Organize practice with a **practice routine**. Do not be reluctant to use a clock to help adhere to a schedule. When there is less time to practice on a given day, try to approach every item in the routine, but in smaller increments of time. "Building time" and "performing time" will need to be altered when there are upcoming performances.

6. ALWAYS **listen** to what is coming out of the violin. Expect every next note. Be able to identify every note that does not meet expectations. Ask "why". Seek solutions, and never give up! A convincing performance cannot be given with shaky intonation or sloppy bow technique.

7. Always **imagine** the sound before putting bow to string, and expect every twist and turn of a phrase.

8. **Imagination** and **curiosity** are two of the greatest and most personal tools. They have the power to create a distinctive voice that will be long remembered.

9. **Preparation** builds confidence.

10. Be able to start on any note of a piece you are studying, and memorize **landmarks**.

11. Try to eliminate the drudgery of practice by staying fresh and inspired. ALWAYS say something with your playing. Have a **vision** of your goals during every moment of your practice. Remember to recognize your accomplishments even if they are small, and have **faith** that every positive step is taking you closer to your **dreams**.

12. **Slow Practice = Fast Progress!**

Appendix II

IMPROVING INTONATION THROUGH THE "STOP BOW" METHOD

Throughout my many years of performing and teaching, I have found that probably the most frequently experienced frustration with our instrument lies in the difficulties we face with INTONATION. If violins came with frets or keys, a great many problems encountered by violinists would be solved. Obviously, this not being the case, we need to develop strategies that make traversing the fingerboard as comfortable and dependable as possible.

One of the most common but oddly overlooked deterrents to secure intonation is actually quite simple. It is very easy not to listen! With a piano, all of the notes are laid out in front of us. In fact, we sit right above them. Intonation is not an issue, so listening to the sounds we produce and creating musical ideas is a much more natural process. This, unfortunately, is not the case with the violin. Our instrument is simply not comfortable. We can try to give it more physical ease by attaching devices and learning relaxation skills, but the bottom line is that holding this piece of wood between our heads and collar bones with twisted arms can only reach a moderate comfort level that in itself varies with each individual. Because our attempts at achieving a sense of naturalness with regard to posture take so much effort and because our basic technique requires an ever increasing knowledge of how to cope with inherent discomforts, our minds are not always focused on the most important element of intonation, which is, of course…listening. All of this, when coupled with the desire to complete tasks as quickly as possible, makes it quite a challenge to achieve the highest quality playing in the most effortless way. This is why I feel that the "Stop Bow" method is one of the most valuable tools we can use in developing the patience and discipline required to develop the mastery of our art. Saving time seems to be increasingly critical given the myriads of activities and responsibilities we encounter every day. Here is an easy method by which efficient practice can become a part of our daily lives.

The "Stop Bow Method," which I first encountered in its purest form at the School for Strings in New York City, can be applied to shifting and the improvement of **intonation**. Used in a broader sense, it may also be employed to encourage attentive listening for the development of the musical concepts of phrasing, direction and line.

APPLICATION OF THE "STOP BOW METHOD" TO SHIFTING

Practice back and forth between the two notes of the shift:

1. slowly with stops;

2. faster with stops;

3. slowly with smooth bows;

4. faster with smooth bows

IMPLEMENTATION OF THE "STOP BOW METHOD" IN THE IMPROVEMENT OF INTONATION (AND IN GENERAL PRACTICE)

1. Play the open string on which the note in question resides.

2. Stop.

3. Hear the next note in your mind's ear.

4. Stop.

5. Play the corrected note, matching what you have heard.

6. Stop. Analyze the result. When focusing on intonation, it is best to RESIST HUNTING for the correct note. Instead, use inner speech to make a judgment as to whether the note in question is right on target, too high, or too low.

> Probably the most frequently neglected step of the analysis process is the most obvious. Simply ask, "Why?" Asking why something is not working, or, for that matter, why it *is* working is guaranteed to accelerate the learning process. Two of the greatest secrets to efficient practice lie in the realizations that, if a problem persists, seeking its cause will shorten its duration. *And, if one solution does not work, with imagination, the other possibilities are boundless.*

7. Repair or reinforce as needed by repeating the process with the possible solution in mind. (When discovered, be sure to immediately reinforce the correct result at least three times in a row for security.) Understand that quite often, an over-compensation will take place first. Developing the patience it takes to employ this method is almost as important as the method itself. Taking the time to imagine and expect every note, both accurately and in its musical context, will help build a foundation for artistic excellence. REMEMBER: Repetition without thought, otherwise known as playing by "rote," often tends to reinforce habits that will only have to be corrected in the future. Why waste that kind of time?

Appendix III

SOUNDING POINT

UNDERLYING PRINCIPLE

The Sounding Point is the place on the string that gives the best sound for a particular bow stroke. It is affected by the desired speed and weight of the bow stroke as well as the thickness of each string.

FORMAL DIRECTIONS

Formal directions serve to establish the most dependable method for the study of sounding points. With this approach, it is possible for you to discover and reinforce the concepts of movement from one sounding point to another. At first, the angles made with the bow to enact these changes will be highly exaggerated. When the sounding point changes required by basic bow strokes are able to be handled in this fashion, the angles can be lessened until they are hardly noticeable. With patience and perseverance the use of formal directions can help to develop a secure sense of bow control that is well worth the effort!

TERMINOLOGY

The term "directions" applies to the placement of the bow hand as well as the angles in which the bow will move. "Out" refers to the direction that pulls or places your hand (and the bow) away from the bridge. "In" is the direction that pulls or places your bow hand (and bow) closer to the bridge.

GETTING STARTED

Always use open strings first for all combinations. Find the sounding point for a light martelé. Listen carefully to make this determination. Decide what sounds best for the particular speed and articulation of this stroke. Because of their speed, martelés sound better away from the bridge. Practice them, for this purpose, with straight bows in the upper half until they are consistent in articulation, weight and speed.

Next, find the sounding point for a slower bow, such as a two-note slur. Practice slow, straight bows (imagining the two-note slur) without diminuendos in the upper half of the bow on the slur sounding point which will be closer to the bridge. A mixed bowing pattern of three eighth notes (one down and two slurred up) will be used to begin. (See Mixed Bowings chart.) As bow control develops, add more and more notes to the up bow slurs. This will increase the challenge of keeping the sound by staying on the sounding point. When this exercise is consistently successful, practice all of the following mixed bowing combinations from the Mixed Bowings Chart on your scales.

When you are ready, move on.

THE FAMOUS FOUR

Here are four basic combinations that will give you the greatest benefit from formal directions.

1. Martelé and legato (otherwise known as "preparation" because this is the most basic way to prepare for sounding point changes)

2. Detaché and legato

3. Spiccato and legato

4. Spiccato and spiccato.

Practice all of these combinations on open strings first using the Mixed Bowings Chart.

APPLICATION OF FORMAL DIRECTIONS FOR BOW CONTROL (SEE MIXED BOWINGS CHART)

Start the three-eighth note patterns with down bows first. (Each combination can be started on an up or down bow for further exploration. Because sounding points will reverse, so will the bow directions.) Here are the formal directions for the "Famous Four" which are the four most common combinations of bow strokes to be used for this purpose. Remember that exaggeration and slow, careful work will result in a dependable control of the bow that will affect everything played, from scales to etude-caprices to short pieces and master concerti.

1. (Preparation) martelé and legato (1 note separate, 2 notes slurred): start slightly away from the bridge; pull "out" with hand on the down bow martelé, so the tip arrives closer to bridge. The bow has moved to the sounding point of the next slur! Then stay "out" with the hand so the contact point (place where the bow contacts string) remains on the sounding point for the up bow slur. Add a little extra weight to the slow up bow slur to balance the sound of the faster martelé stroke. Divide the upper half of the bow accurately in order to avoid an undesirable diminuendo. The goal is to be able to play three even sounding notes with two different bow strokes. Listen carefully to determine if you have pulled out too far. This will be easy to hear and feel because the sound will not be pure and the bow will skid. Correct this by lessening the angle. However, always be sure that each end of the bow starts and finishes on the appropriate sounding point. If the bow has stayed "out," it should have ended on the martelé sounding point, ready for the next stroke. "Preparation" is the most exaggerated of all combinations. When this has been mastered at a slow tempo with a consistently crisp, fast, and relatively light martelé, move on.

2. Detaché and legato: The sounding point changes for these strokes are much the same as those for the martelé and legato combination, but the angles are less. Practice slowly and with great care in the upper half of the bow. When consistent, increase the tempo. Always use the ear as the judge for sounding point placement. The detaché stroke is not as fast as a martelé. Its distance from the bridge will be determined by its speed. The faster the detaché, the farther away from the bridge it will need to be. ("Out" and "stay out" will still be used with discretion depending on the speed.)

3. Spiccato and legato: The bow directions for this combination are still the same as they were for martelé and legato, but this is a diminutive version using a concentrated amount of bow at its balance point (a place just below the middle where spiccatos work best). Once again, listen carefully to find the sounding point for spiccato. For this exercise, both spiccatos and legatos will use approximately the same amount of bow. Obviously, here the bow directions will have to be quite minimal. Keep the sounding points in mind and always try to achieve the most ringing, natural spiccato. Remember to have flexible fingers. Drop the bow well, and let it do the work. The up bow slurs will feel like the "brake" is being put on, but keep the bow moving and stay slightly "out" so the slur will remain on its sounding point and give the best sound. When comfortable and successful with this combination, gradually increase the speed while keeping all notes even.

4. Spiccato and spiccato: With formal directions in the back of your mind, find the sounding point for the spiccato strokes. For this combination, all notes will be spiccato and depend on the flexibility of the hand and fingers. Approach the slur with a series of retakes, or allow it to travel a small distance in the neighborhood of the bow's balance point. Let the bow drop and do the work itself with the guidance of the fingers and slight motion of the forearm. Always listen for a resonant sound.

To practice using sounding points for bow control, apply the "Famous Four" to Section II of the Mixed Bowings Chart.

MIXED BOWINGS CHART

(Practice these figures in the upper half of the bow. To compensate for the differences in bow speeds, play lighter on the separate notes and heavier on the slurs. Balance the sounds of the different strokes proportionally.)

Formal directions for the mixed bowings below would be as follows:
(Repeat each figure with thought.)

SECTION 1

Out; Stay out.   **In; Stay in.**

 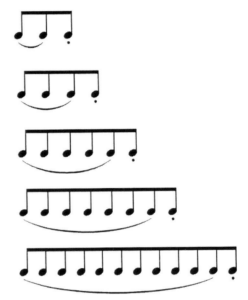

SECTION 2

In; Straight; Out; Stay out; Straight; In

Out; Stay out; Straight; In; Stay in; Straight

Straight; In; Stay in; Straight; Out; Stay out

(NOTE: When separate notes appear back to back, the first of the two will be straight because it is already on the sounding point. The second will prepare for the sounding point of the next note.)

APPENDIX IV

RHYTHMS

The use of rhythms in the practice of passage work is an invaluable tool for developing ACCURACY, COORDINATION, SECURITY and MENTAL ALERTNESS. Furthermore, their usage encourages THINKING AHEAD.

Be able to count the rhythms below aloud with syllables. Also be able to play and count these rhythms aloud simultaneously. (For many, two rhythmic groups will constitute a measure.) When solid, build these rhythms on scales, organizing the bow to accommodate increasing numbers of groups. (e.g. the first 2/4 rhythm can be played with 1, 2, 3, 4 and 6 groups of notes per bow.)

Rhythmic reversals are particularly effective in curing technical difficulties. With logic, choose rhythms that are the most challenging for the particular passage needing improvement. They will be most beneficial.

Count these subdivisions aloud to a slow beat before playing. (e.g. "1-2; 1-2-3-4-, 1-2-3-4-5-6-")

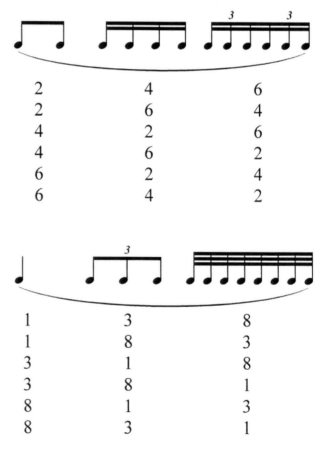

2	4	6
2	6	4
4	2	6
4	6	2
6	2	4
6	4	2

1	3	8
1	8	3
3	1	8
3	8	1
8	1	3
8	3	1

With many thanks to Ivan Galamian and Margaret Pardee, as these rhythms were derived from their teachings.

APPENDIX V

DOUBLE STOP STRATEGIES

When practicing double stops, listen for RESULTANT tones. These "ghost notes", made by the combination of two notes, are actually heard by the inner ear as a third tone. The jury is still out as to whether 3rd tones are "psycho-acoustical phenomenae" or the result of mathematical equations. But famed violinist and composer Giuseppi Tartini (1692–1770) is known to have been the first to have used the identification of these third notes (also referred to as "Tartini Tones") as a tool in the correction of faulty double stop intonation, and they continue to intrigue many a violinist seeking to improve in this area today.

To hear an example of a resultant tone, play on the A and E strings with a 1st and 2nd finger respectively: B and G. With resultant tones, a "buzz" may be audible first. However, with careful listening, this buzz will often transform into a pitch that can be identified. In this case, the pitch that will most likely become audible is a "D" which is the 5th of the chord.

Some resultant tones are easier to hear and identify than others. Recognition of these pitches is by no means the only way to attain accuracy with double stops. Listed below are some more suggestions for the practice of double stops.

1. Know intervals and their qualities, both vertically (for individual chords) and horizontally (between chords).

2. Glissandi are effective tools for the learning and reinforcement of intervallic distances.

3. Practice sounding one note while fingering the other in order to give individual attention to the placement of each. Reverse.

4. Make major intervals more major and minor intervals more minor (e.g., thinking across the strings, to make major 3rds more major, narrow the distance between fingers, but with major 6ths, widen the distance slightly).

5. Practice back and forth between pairs of double stops, recognizing intervals both vertically and horizontally. Use stop bow work for time to think between playing consecutive double stops. With inner speech, identify notes that are not in tune. Determine how and *why*. Use imagination to develop a strategy for fixing problems permanently. If one tactic does not work, try another.

APPENDIX VI

CHORDS

1. With the bow in hand and relaxed fingers, practice large counter-clockwise circles above the strings. Curve fingers when approaching the frog, and gradually relax them when leaving. (This can be practiced without the bow, too.) At the bottom of the circle, start away from the bridge where strings are less arched. Pull slightly "in" (towards bridge) with the upper arm since the sounding points of the lower strings are farther away from the bridge than those of the upper strings. Keep the bow moving.

2. Practice four-note chords first on open string equivalents. To begin, start from the air and practice the lower two notes only. Keep moving the bow while approaching the G and D strings. (Think of the most experienced jet pilot making the most unnoticeable landing. No sudden jolts, stops or extra weight should interfere with the pulling of these two notes.) Use about 1/3 of the bow. Try to get the richest, most resonant sound by listening and watching the strings vibrate. Circle around, repeating over and over until there is no crunch. Remember to pull slightly "in" using the upper arm. If the angle "in" is too steep, straighten the bow by pulling slightly "out" (away from bridge) at the place above the middle where the stick begins to curve.

3. When the above steps are dependable, repeat step 2, but this time, stop almost imperceptibly (i.e. without pressing) after using 1/3 of bow. Drop your elbow to the level appropriate for the two upper note equivalents (A and E strings) and pull the bow to its tip, pronating slightly in order to keep the bow in the string. (Pronating is like turning a doorknob. The forearm rotates counter-clockwise, and the bow hair will flatten as a result.) Circle around and repeat over and over making improvements on each repetition.

4. When step 3 is successful at least 3 times in a row and the bow is well organized, practice without stops, still remaining on open strings. (The breaking of a chord is dependent on its character. Some will be broken more definitely than others. Some will anticipate the beat, while others may be placed slightly closer to the fingerboard where there is less of an arch to achieve a more organ-like effect.) For all chords, maintain the goals mentioned in step 2.

5. When all of the above steps are functioning well, find a sample chord such as the first chord in the Mozart etude-caprice. Take the time to tune the B-flat of this chord with its neighboring open D before starting. Then make sure the interval of the 6th (B-flat to G) is perfectly in tune. (See Appendix V for tips on double stops.) When this is accomplished, repeat steps 3 and 4 with the notes from the chord. Finally, when the chord sounds easy and open…add vibrato.

6. (Three-note chords) Lifting the elbow almost unnoticeably, after the middle of the bow, and playing where the strings are more level (i.e. closer to the fingerboard) will help three-note chords sound all at once.

7. **A few reminders**: Keep the bow moving while making circles. Remember to start the stroke with the upper arm (shoulder down) and open your inside elbow approximately where the stick begins to curve. Also remember to curve fingers when approaching the frog, relaxing them afterwards. Use the springs in your hand and a relaxed bow arm to pull the warmest sound for chords.

COMPOSERS' BIOGRAPHIES

Antonio Vivaldi

Not long after being ordained a priest, Italian composer Antonio Vivaldi (1678–1741) refused to say Mass. It is not known whether this was due to his poor health or an intense desire to completely immerse himself in his music. Referred to as "the red-headed priest" by his great admirer, J.S. Bach, Vivaldi is remembered as one of the most prominent and prolific composers of the late Baroque period. Hired as music director of the Ospedale della Pieta, a girls' orphanage in Venice, Vivaldi remained connected with this school for over thirty years, writing many of his compositions for its residents. Composer of numerous operas, theater pieces and choral works, he is best known for having written over 550 concertos. His rhythmic vitality, use of sequences, and distinctive method of blending solo with orchestral material make Vivaldi's music immediately recognizable.

Johann Sebastian Bach

Considered by many to have been the greatest composer of all time, Johann Sebastian Bach (1685–1750) was not only a renowned German keyboard virtuoso, but also an accomplished violinist and violist. His keyboard works show the influence of the string family in their attention to phrasing and color, while his string writing was obviously affected by his love of polyphony (music with more than one voice, or part, of equal importance). A prolific composer, J.S. Bach wrote thousands of compositions, many for the churches where he was employed, others as instructional material for his teaching. His sacred and secular works for chorus and orchestra, in addition to his writing for solo instruments, brought the music of the Baroque period to its artistic summit.

George Frideric Handel

Although German born, English Baroque composer, George Frideric Handel (1685–1759) may be best known for his creation of English Oratorio. He made significant contributions to every type of vocal and instrumental music prevalent during his lifetime. The effect of Handel's theatrical writing on all of his compositions is evident in his wide variety of expression. His string writing contrasts boldness, majesty and energy with warm, passionate lyricism. Handel's influence was deeply felt by such composers as Bach, Haydn, Mozart, Beethoven and Mendelssohn. Due in part to the revival of original baroque performance practice, much of his music, particularly in the genre of opera, is being rediscovered and enjoyed again today.

Joseph Haydn

Credited with having been the "father of the string quartet," Joseph Haydn (1732–1809), Austrian composer, freed the viola and cello from their former accompanimental roles, and provided inspiration to all subsequent composers of quartet literature. His innovative work in the realm of symphonies was of equal importance, and much of his vocal writing was considered masterful. Known for his amiable and fun-loving personality, his love of pranks often found its way into his compositions. Only for a brief time, the personality of his writing darkened with the emotional intensity influenced by the romantic tendencies of the Sturm und Drang movement in literature. "Papa Haydn" began his career as an employee of the courts and ended it as a musical hero.

Wolfgang Amadeus Mozart

In his brief lifetime, the Austrian composer, Wolfgang Amadeus Mozart (1756–1791) wrote over 600 compositions encompassing all musical genres and representing the epitome of Classical style. A child prodigy already experiencing success as a performer and composer by the age of five, he was introduced to the royalty through numerous concert tours. As Mozart matured, his skills as a pianist and composer of operas and instrumental works brought him great popularity in European society. His love for operatic characters permeated his writing and much like his life, contrasted light-hearted innocence with soulful passion. Sadly, although the profound impact he has had on generations of musicians and composers is unquestionable, during his lifetime, Mozart never enjoyed the patronage he deserved, and his life ended prematurely in poverty and despair.

Ludwig van Beethoven

Prone to fits of temper, derived in large part from an unfortunate upbringing and ill health, the music of German composer, Ludwig van Beethoven (1770–1827) manifests many of the same characteristics of his varied personality. Bridging the ideals of the Classic and Romantic periods, his earlier compositions faithfully adhered to the forms of Handel, Mozart and Bach while, later in life, impending deafness and withdrawal from society played a significant role in his transition to more progressive and individualistic musical thought. Harmonic innovations, sudden contrasts in dynamics, and dramatic shifts in emotional intensity reflected his increasing desire to seek refuge in his art. In so doing, Beethoven gave voice to a new era and became one of the most influential composers in the history of music.

Niccolo Paganini

Accused of being "in league with the devil" as a result of the superhuman feats Niccolo Paganini (1782–1840) could accomplish on the violin, this Italian virtuoso's life has become legendary. From his earliest years, Paganini favored the use of theme and variations as a method of displaying his talent and imagination. Double stops, harmonics, left hand pizzicato, to mention a few devices, added brilliance to his writing. Suffering from a disease with symptoms thought to have affected his appearance and joint extensibility, his extraordinary abilities and demeanor captivated the crowds, while the pyrotechnics of his compositions continue to provide challenges to even the greatest of violinists today.

Johannes Brahms

Johannes Brahms (1833–1897), German composer of the Romantic period, felt compelled to live up to a prediction and public announcement by his friend, the highly esteemed Robert Schumann. Extolled as "the coming hero among composers," Brahms was a perfectionist who was very selective in choosing works he would release to the public and often took years to be sure they could not be improved. His *German Requiem* established his fame, but he is well known for his symphonies, concerti, chamber music, piano works, and songs. Unlike many of his contemporaries, Brahms' compositions reflect his deep admiration for the ideals of the classical period and breathe new life into the older forms. A romantic at heart, it may, however, have been his love of the new capabilities of the modern piano that inspired the rich sonorities in his writing.

Pablo de Sarasate

Recognized for his impeccable technique and musicianship, the Spanish violinist, Pablo de Sarasate (1844–1908) charmed his audiences with his pure, sweet tone, elegant manner and striking appearance. His compositions, often based on popular operas, showcased Spanish melodies and rhythms. A prolific composer, Sarasate's writings generally fall into five categories: folk-inspired pieces, opera fantasies, original works, transcriptions and cadenzas. It is without a doubt that European composers of the day were highly influenced by Sarasate's distinctive style. Many composers dedicated works to the Spanish virtuoso whose own exciting pieces continue to delight audiences in the recitals of students and concert artists to this day.

Maurice Ravel

French Impressionist composer, Maurice Ravel (1875–1937) used a palette of instrumental colors to paint imaginative piano, vocal and chamber works, as well as his rich orchestrations. Influenced by his mother's Spanish lullabies, European folk songs, Asian music, American jazz and classical mythology, Maurice Ravel's poignant melodies often appear in exotic and colorful settings. Nicknamed the "Swiss Watchmaker" by Stravinsky because of his father's Swiss background and Maurice's meticulous care for form and detail, Ravel's musical output was relatively small. However, more than half of his compositions remain favorites on concert programs.

Bela Bartok

The music of Bela Bartok (1881–1945) contains exotic rhythms, harmonies and scales that he discovered by collecting and examining thousands of examples of folk music from remote parts of his native Hungary and surrounding countries. Bartok was a gifted pianist and often performed his own compositions on his concert tours. In addition to piano literature, his colorful writings include works for violin, viola, chamber ensembles and orchestra. His deep love of the simple life combined with a strong belief in reality eventually inspired his withdrawal from the public. Ridiculed by those who did not understand his music, or feel its nationalistic intent, Bartok's "new voice" has become popular only after his death.

Aaron Copland

Aaron Copland (1900–1990) conveyed a new and distinctive American voice with the imagination and simplicity he infused into his compositions. Copland's works are most noted in the genres of ballet, opera and film. It has been said that his use of octaves, open harmonies and American folk songs evoke the landscape of America. Influential in the genre of film music, he was innovative by employing music to purposefully delineate the actors' thoughts and intensify emotions by subtle means. A shy and modest man, Aaron Copland developed a new twentieth century language that he hoped to use to communicate serious music to a broad audience.

BIBLIOGRAPHY

Ammer, Christine. *Harper's Dictionary of Music*, Harper & Row Publishers (New York, 1973)

Apel, Willi. *The Harvard Brief Dictionary of Music*, Pocket Books (New York, 1960)

Autexier, Philippe A. *Beethoven, The Composer as Hero*, Harry N. Abrams, Inc. (New York, 1992)

Butterworth, Neil. *Haydn, his life and times*, Midas Books (Kent, U.K. 1977)

Campbell, Margaret. *The Great Violinists*, Doubleday & Company, Inc. (New York, 1981)

Copland, Aaron. *Music and Imagination*, Harvard University Press (Massachusetts, 1977)

Dart, Thurston. *The Interpretation of Music*, Harper & Row, Publishers (New York, 1954)

Donington, Robert. *String Playing in Baroque Music*, Faber Music Ltd. (London, 1977)

Elson, Louis C. (ed.). *Modern Music and Musicians*, Vol. 2, The University Society, Inc. (New York, 1912)

Fisk, Josiah (ed.). *Composers on Music, Eight Centuries of Writings*, Northeastern University Press (Boston, 1997)

Fleming, William. *Arts and Ideas*, Holt, Rinehart and Winston, Inc. (New York, 1974)

Flesch, Carl. *Art of Violin Playing: Book One*, Carl Fischer, Inc. (Boston, 1926)

Galamian, Ivan. *Principles of Violin Playing and Teaching*, Prentice-Hall (New Jersey, 1962)

Galewitz, Herb (ed.). *Music, A Book of Quotations*, Dover Publications, Inc. (New York, 2001)

Krehbiel, Henry Edward (ed.). *Beethoven: The Man and the Artist*, as Revealed in his Own Words, Dover Publications, Inc. (New York, 1965)

Krehbiel, Henry Edward (ed.). *Mozart: The Man and the Artist Revealed in his Own Words*, Dover Publications, Inc. (New York, 1965)

Mason, Daniel Gregory (ed.). *Masters in Music*, Vol. 5, Bates and Guild Company (Boston, 1905)

Moore, Douglas. *A Guide to Musical Styles*, W.W. Norton & Company, Inc. (New York, 1962)

Osborne, Charles (ed.). *The Dictionary of Composers*, Taplinger Publishing Company (New York, 1981)

Remy, Alfred (ed.). *Baker's Biographical Dictionary of Musicians*, G.Schirmer Inc. (New York, 1900)

Roth, Henry. *Violin Virtuosos from Paganini to the 21st Century*, California Classics, (Los Angeles, 1997)

Sadie, Stanley (ed.). *The New Grove Dictionary of Music and Musicians*, Macmillan Publishers (New York, 2001)

Scherman, Thomas K. (ed.). *The Beethoven Companion, A Comprehensive guide to Beethoven – his life and work*, Doubleday & Company, Inc. (New York, 1972)

Schweitzer, Albert. *J.S.Bach, 2 vols*, Dover Publications (New York, 1966)

Shapiro, Nat (ed.). *An Encyclopedia of Quotations About Music*, Da Capo Press (New York, 1978)

Sonneck, O.G. (ed.). *Beethoven, Impressions by his Contemporaries*, Dover Publications, Inc. (New York, 1967)

Wold, Milo. *An Introduction to Music and Art in the Western World*, Wm. C. Brown Company Publishers (Iowa, 1975)

http://ehistory.osu.edu/osu/timeline/timeline.cfm?Era_id=12

http://ehistory.osu.edu/world/TimeLineDisplay.cfm?Era_id=13

http://en.wikipedia.org/wiki/Timeline_of_United_States_history_(1950-1969)

http://timelines.ws/countries/AUSTRIA.HTML

http://wiki.answers.com/

http://www.britannica.com/

http://www.cbn.com/spirituallife/ChurchAndMinistry/ChurchHistory/Historical_Timeline_1000-1999.aspx

http://www.facts-about.org.uk/history-and-events-timeline-austrian.htm

http://www.fsmitha.com/time19-6.htm

http://www.history-timelines.org.uk/places-timelines/27-italy-history-timeline.htm

http://www.wikipedia.org/

http://www.wikimedia.org

Etude-Caprice in the Style of Bach used by permission of Black Squirrel Publishing from *Reflections from the Edge of the Millennium for Violin Alone* by Amy Barlowe.

Notes

AMY BARLOWE

AMY BARLOWE, violinist and composer, received her B.M. and M.M. degrees from the Juilliard School after studies with Ivan Galamian and Margaret Pardee. Her chamber music coaches include Josef Gingold, Felix Galimir, Samuel Rhodes and Earl Carlyss.

She is the recipient of numerous awards including the Helena Rubinstein Scholarship, Atkinson and Northwest Area grants. Her critically acclaimed solo recitals and chamber music performances have taken her throughout the United States, Canada, and Mexico, as well as to the major concert halls of New York City. Josef Gingold praised her for "...fine musicianship, excellent instrumental qualities, and a devotion to all things musical." Ms. Barlowe has been featured on PM Magazine, performed as guest artist on numerous radio stations, and toured extensively throughout the Northwest as violinist of the Oregon Trio.

In 1988, she and her husband, Alan Bodman, formed the Duo [AB]2 (AB-squared). They have recorded for the Medici and Azica labels. *"Their tonal production is flawless, and musically they meet the highest standards."* – American Record Guide

Ms. Barlowe's original compositions and arrangements include works for two violins and piano, an opera ballet, and a Requiem Mass. Her two Celtic duos for two violas, appear on a CD recorded by the Aureole Trio and have been released on the Koch International label. Most recently, Ms. Barlowe's arrangement of "Schindler's List" for two violins and piano received the endorsement of John Williams and has been published for two violins or violin and viola with orchestra by Hal Leonard.

Formerly Associate Professor of Violin at Willamette University in Salem, Oregon, Ms. Barlowe has held teaching positions at the Juilliard Pre-College and New York's School for Strings, as well as the Estherwood and Bowdoin Summer Music Festivals. Currently, she is on the artist/faculty of the Meadowmount School of Music and the Ohio Conservatory. She has founded a vibrant new chamber orchestra called Akron Baroque.

Ms. Barlowe's biography has been listed in *Who's Who in America, Who's Who in American Women*, and the 2010 edition of *Who's Who in the World*.